Mindful of Others

Teaching Children to Teach

Suzanne Brady

Monte Vista School
Monterey, California

and

Suzie Jacobs

University of Hawaii
Honolulu, Hawaii

HEINEMANN
Portsmouth, NH

HEINEMANN
A division of Reed Elsevier Inc.
361 Hanover Street
Portsmouth, NH 03801–3912
Offices and agents throughout the world

Every effort has been made to contact the copyright holders for permission to reprint borrowed material where necessary. We regret any oversights that may have occurred and would be happy to rectify them in future printings of this work.

Library of Congress Cataloging-in-Publication Data

Brady, Suzanne.
   Mindful of others : teaching children to teach / Suzanne Brady and Suzie Jacobs.
      p.   cm.
   Includes bibliographical references and index.
   ISBN 0-435-08356-2 (alk. paper)
   1. Teaching.   2. Teacher-student relationships.   3. Dialogue—
Study and teaching.   4. Group work in education.   5. Language arts.
6. Reading.   I. Jacobs, Suzie.   II. Title.
LB1025.3.B73   1994
371.1'02—dc20   93–48126
                                                                CIP

Editor: Toby R. Gordon
Production: Melissa L. Inglis
Text Design: George McLean
Cover Design: Catherine Hawkes
Photos by Daniel Rico

Printed in the United States of America on acid-free paper
99 98 97 96 95 94 EB 1 2 3 4 5 6 7

To Don Rothman

Contents

Preface

In the summer of 1982, I joined thirty-nine other teachers from all over the country for a week in the uplands of Maui on the side of the volcano Haleakala. They were teachers of all academic levels. We enjoyed good talk, good food, interesting presentations, and performances of authentic hula and Hawaiian chanting. We had time for the beach and time for writing. This was the Maui Writing Project Symposium.

Halfway into the week, when all forty of us were pretty well acquainted, Professor Suzie Jacobs of the University of Hawaii made her presentation. I remember sitting in the breezy meeting room after lunch, waiting for the session to start but feeling the beginnings of an afternoon nap. I reminded myself that I'd come for substance as well as slumber and that I needed to be alert. Suzie and I had already swapped stories of our teen-age children. Hers had grown up in Honolulu, mine in Carmel. We shared an interest in children's language. So I sat up straight, pencil poised, to take good notes.

Suzie talked about children's writing. What happens *as* children write. *Too* much. Their minds must juggle ten balls at once. But it's exciting. Complexity is exciting. Complexity comes from choosing. I thought about my fifth graders, who wrote rambling stories with too many characters and not enough plot. Said Suzie, teachers sometimes "save" children from complexity to ensure neatness and good spelling.

Then she said, "Remember the value of chaos. The job of the teacher is to create chaos and the job of the students is to bring order to it." My chair jumped. What an arresting idea! Chaos doesn't have to be negative. Chaos might be the momentary confusion that leads a mind to wake up and go to work, to clear a path and make sense. Chaos can lead plodders to dance.

I remember searching Suzie out, making sure we were on the same van to the beach, eating at the same table. When we began to talk, I began picking her brain, gathering all the insight I could in the few days we had left. I think I expected another presentation tailored to my questions, but this didn't happen. She countered my questions with her own, always asking *why*. Why do you do this or that in school? On the last day, instead of saying, "Have a safe trip home," she wanted to know what *else* was going on with my fifth graders. Her questions made me realize that I wasn't that sure. I wanted to continue this conversation.

Back in my Monterey classroom, I reflected on my teaching with Suzie always at the edge of my mind. We managed to meet at conferences. She came to California to join me in summer workshops for the Central California Writing Project. I went to Hawaii for "vacation." We collaborated on an article for *Language Arts* (Jacobs 1984) and a chapter in Newkirk and Atwell's *Understanding Writing* (Brady and Jacobs 1988). Years passed.

At some point, Suzie began talking book. At a conversation's high point she'd say, "We really ought to write this down." The very thought was appalling. I already had a full-time job with very little energy left over. Conversation was one thing, writing it down quite another.

Suzie persisted. "Some day," I'd counter. I knew I was too busy, but I also remembered that the act of writing engenders new thought. I had welcomed chaos. Perhaps Suzie and I could bring about some order.

We began to write this book.

Suzanne Brady

On the third day of the five-day Maui conference, as I stood in the lunch line, I heard Suzanne laugh. The rest of us had been talking about the surprising things our students say, when this laugh launched her into a story about eight- and nine-year-olds and how differently they think.

"I remember a couple of years ago," she said, "when I had a combination third-fourth grade. At the front of the room a fourth grader,

Yuki, was giving her talk on stars—how the sun was really a star, and how hot they were, and so on. Well, it was Christmas time and one bright third grader, who must have just finished decorating his tree at home, raised his hand at question time. With an absolutely straight face," and here Suzanne raised her hand and mimicked the earnest look of a third grader, "this child asked, 'What about the stars with points?'"

"The fourth graders couldn't believe their ears," said Suzanne. "They turned around and just stared at this child. But the *third* graders all looked at Yuki, and they were nodding as if to say, 'Yeaaahhh! What about the ones with points?'"

What difference did age make in these children's perceptions of stars, and what other mysteries of the mind could this woman with the laugh reveal? If I could talk with her long enough, I thought, I'd have a window on language and thought. As an applied linguist, I knew that language was basic to thought. Certain *types* of thought were acquired in school. But what school? What kind of classroom, and what kind of classroom language?

At the Maui symposium there was time for only snatches of talk with Suzanne, right up until the last day. Then, when everyone else had left, I finally got my chance. We sat by the pool, talking about chaos. Suzanne said that some administrators worried about chaos, especially when teachers clamored for change in the curriculum. I said that some of my university students resisted attempts to bring new material into their essays, saying, "I don't want to mess up what I've got." Suzanne said she understood my students' apprehensions. Sometimes she would say sternly to herself: "This is not Summerhill. If I give ten-year-old children all this choice, am I going to invite more chaos than I can handle?" The conversation stayed with me for days, playing itself back at odd moments in my head.

As soon as I returned to Honolulu, I checked out the educational video, *Flight* (Brady 1982), in which Suzanne appeared as a model teacher of writing. I saw a classful of children using writing as a way into reading and talking. One child studied the flight of birds by learning how their wings were shaped, another took a flight in a small airplane and interviewed the pilot, and another studied the aerodynamics of paper airplanes. What had drawn me to talk to Suzanne was also drawing these children into conversation: they had questions to ask.

For both the children and ourselves, conversation is a way of making sense of things in the company of peers. Writing this book seems to us a natural way to extend a conversation to others.

By 1990, eight years after Maui, many of our friends and colleagues had joined our conversation about teaching. We gratefully acknowledge those who helped us convert these words from speech to print. In Honolulu, Lena Jacobs, Marilyn Kim, Tomi Knaefler, and Roger Whitlock listened and commented. Alison Adams, Ann Bayer, Elizabeth Brandt, Paula Levin, and Karen Watson-Gegeo identified problems in theory. University colleagues in Oregon, Duncan Carter, Carol Franks, and Barbara Weiss, read drafts with care and insight, as did Bernice Jakel, Kay Wiseman, and Barbara Snepp of Southport Elementary in Indianapolis. We thank Lisa Meckel for asking questions and the other Central California Writing Project members for listening to our early efforts: Jeff Arnett, Debbie Bell, Roger Bunch, Robin Drury, Virginia Draper, Ellen Hart, Adrienne Jerman, Patty Lockett, Nancy Matlock, Sylvia Mendez, Sarah-Hope Parmeter, Don Rothman, Rebecca Salinas, Ruby Vazquez, Lucia Villareal, Tomasita Villareal, and Karen Warren. We also thank our California colleagues Jane Boehle, Patty Brimie, Yvonne Despard, Ellen Maupin, and Dorothy Petitt. To Marilyn Woods goes a special thanks.

Thanks to the principals and faculties of Monte Vista School and Del Monte School, the children who enliven these pages, and their parents. Thanks also to educator Bill Honig, for his vision and leadership. Finally we thank our husbands, James Brady and Roderick Jacobs, for being cooks, editors, and general support. This book could not have been done without them.

Suzie Jacobs

Introduction

All the way back to Greek antiquity, teachers have said that learning should be dialogic. Schoolroom knowledge is brought to life by conversational exchange.

But John Goodlad and his team of observers found little dialogue in the thirty-eight schools they visited in the early 1980s. "The classroom," concludes Goodlad, "is a constrained and constraining environment" (1984, 109). Teachers are engaged most of the time in "either frontal teaching, monitoring students' seat work, or conducting quizzes." Rarely do students learn from one another. Rarely do they initiate interaction with the teacher (1984, 124). Both students and teachers, says Goodlad, are fearful of stepping over boundaries. One high school student told the investigators, "We're birds in a cage. The door is open, but there's a cat just outside." Students are not the only ones who feel constrained. Teachers, says Goodlad, are right there in the cage with the students.

This book takes up the question such a study poses: Can we make the life of the school more collaborative and more conversational? Can we thereby empower students and teachers?

We begin with the assumption that school will never be more conversational if teachers do not themselves converse. Conversation empowers. Because its structure is invitational—because everybody in a conversation is invited to participate—conversation breaks down the hierarchy that characterizes school relationships: those inside the school, between the school and the downtown administrators, between school districts and universities.

In the process of writing this book, we changed the format from conventional exposition to dialogue, mainly in response to comments made by our Central California Writing Project colleagues. "What I like most," said Lucia, "is the way you talk, back and forth, a university teacher and an elementary teacher, neither one controlling the other. That relationship is an important part of your statement. Why don't you write this as conversation?" We found the suggestion constructive. As we rewrote, we returned to the transcribed tapes of our original conversations, often writing the language of speech into the text.

Both the style and the content of the book are intended to take on the challenge laid down by Stephen North in his book, *The Making of Knowledge in Composition.* "Practitioners," says North, "need to argue for the value of what they know, and how they come to know it." Too often when teachers write about their practice, the medium of writing itself obscures and misrepresents what was originally an exchange between two people: "I tell you what happened to me, you tell me what happened to you" (1987, 32). Expository writing style highlights particular kinds of logic. The logic of the conversational sort, referred to by North as "experiential-associative," is an essential feature of the knowledge resulting from conversation.

In the course of our conversation in the pages that follow we come to three conclusions:

1. Conversation empowers, especially conversation that asks questions, reflects on experience, and leads the speaker to take action.

2. A teacher conversing with students empowers them by constructing a consciousness of the self as simultaneously intelligent and socially responsible.

3. A teacher can construct these conversations with students in a variety of ways appropriate to writing, reading, and social studies.

As for structure, the book is a series of frames, to use the perspective of Erving Goffman (1972), one frame within another, that frame within still another. Point three above represents the innermost frame: classroom practice. Chapters 4 through 11 show how Suzanne Brady scaffolds a series of conversational, small-group routines, how she came to adopt and shape these routines, and how she continues to evaluate them.

These chapters on classroom practice are set within the larger frame of an argument about consciousness. Chapters 1, 2, and 3 spell out this argument in detail. In a culture where children typically see themselves rank ordered on the basis of individual achievement, and where the means of ordering them this way are suspect at best, teachers can construct an alternative image of the self: an image of each child as a teacher, each contributing to the benefit of others. The consciousness that powerful brains are socially responsive is a theme woven into the rest of the book.

The third frame, the one surrounding the other two, is the argument about the importance of teacher conversation that we've made above. Readers who saw the movie, *My Dinner with Andre*, may remember only vaguely the content of the long conversation between Andre and his friend, but the vision of the two conversants at the dinner table remains sharp in their memories. For those who saw that movie, and for some readers of this book, the nature of the relationship is itself the larger story.

If you, the reader, were here and we had a blackboard, we could draw the frames and talk about all this, but you're not here. For us, the authors, it is not our style to draw frames on the page, though we would be delighted if you were to draw your own picture as a way to think about this point. In our experience, knowledge has too often been laid out, as in teachers' manuals, in schematic drawings. Little circles for the subject areas may surround a large circle enclosing the words in all caps: MEANING-CENTERED CURRICULUM. Ironically, the meaning that goes into the making of such drawings fails to surface on the pages of the manual. The process of making the meaning disappears as the conversation fades.

We hope that no one will consider this book a teachers' manual, that no administrator will hand it down as a directive to be followed. Consider it, please, an invitation to converse.

Ultimately, our purpose is epistemological. We wish to show that knowledge cannot be separated from the means of coming to know. We hope that some of our process still clings to the conclusions we come to and that the activity of our thought remains on the page.

ONE

On Being Smart, Clever, and Intelligent

Suzanne I pull into the parking lot, which is already jammed with yellow buses. Our principal recognizes the car, waves hello, then points to the far corner of the lower playground, which has been opened up for overflow parking. Tomorrow the line of cars will move through and out. Today both parents and kids hurry to check class lists taped to the office window. On the first day of school, children already feel nostalgic about the summer past, but they're also wide-eyed, almost jittery with anticipation. At 7:45 AM of day one, the long carpet of possibility is about to unroll.

I park next to another teacher's pickup truck and turn off the engine, then take a deep breath and a good, calming look at the vast expanse of Monterey Bay. Fog still clings to the top of our mountain. Monte Vista School, "School of the Mountain View."

Last week, while preparing the classroom for the new year, I tacked a poster—I DON'T DO MORNINGS—behind my desk. I yawn, button my sweater, and start across the playground.

"Hi, Mrs. Brady. I'm in your class this year."

"Good morning, Mrs. Brady. Hope you had a good summer."

Whole crowds, it seems, are waiting at the classroom door. Children are on the sidewalk, in the geraniums, perched on the bike rack. (Only four bikes, I notice, for the whole school this morning.)

California kids, here from everywhere. Each year, when they make their ancestor chart for social studies, all the continents but Antarctica are usually represented.

California kids, already making fashion statements with fluorescent latex bicycle shorts and oversize tee shirts. Nick has lines shaved on the sides of his head. He's getting approving looks. Andrea's earrings almost reach her skinny shoulders. (They'll check out my outfits with a critical eye until they hear I'm a grandmother. That lets me off the hook.)

I smile as I unlock the door. "Good morning! Everyone ready for a new year?" With varying cries of joy and reluctance they stream past the welcoming posters made by last year's class on the last day of school.

REMEMBER YOUR HOMEWORK!

DON'T BE A LUMP ON A LOG!

HAVE LOTS OF GOOD FRIENDS!

BE SMART, CLEVER, AND INTELLIGENT!

Suzie As we show later in this chapter, Suzanne begins the school year with an invitation to the children to consider the meaning of *intelligent*. Readers of this book are invited to do the same, especially to consider the ways in which intelligence is tied to identity and serves as a marker of who we are.

I remember, during my childhood, when *intelligence* meant one thing: intelligence quotient or *IQ*. Your IQ was supposed to be a secret, but your mother could find it out from the teacher, and you could weasel it out of your mother. Then you could taunt your friends: "My IQ's higher than yours!" It was terribly important to know in your heart that you had a high IQ. You had something the others didn't have.

Suzanne Nowadays the word is *smart*, rather than *high IQ*. It's important to fifth graders to be smart, although some have already given up trying. *Smart* comes with an institutional stamp of approval, but the word also has a great deal of meaning for children. It's like *high IQ*. It's well known who is and who isn't *smart*, in spite of the fact that teachers don't publicly acknowledge differences.

Smart is almost part of a child's name. "He's Bill. He's Smart." I call the roll on the first day of school: Jimmy Dawson. Michael Flynn. Marisol Flores. Soujanya Rangarao. Then I look around at my collection of California kids and think for a moment. I'm convinced that if I said right now, "Raise your hand if you know whether you're smart or not," almost all the children would put up their hands. Out of thirty, maybe four would look at me and ask, "Smart in what? Smart in math? Smart in reading?" The other twenty-six wouldn't ask questions. They'd know from earlier years that *smart* and *not smart* are words that everybody understands. Everybody in the class could be described by one word or the other.

The ones who see themselves as "smart" often live in fear of losing the label. They actually hold themselves back from taking risks, because who knows, they might fall on their faces. The "not smart" often live in resignation. They may feel there's little chance of ever being smart and that the things they know are somehow not worthy of school.

The children most open to new teaching are the ones not so clearly labeled with this single term. They see themselves as sometimes smart and sometimes not.

Suzie Once your IQ was in place, it stayed there. It didn't move. According to the testing tradition, described by Stephen Gould (1981, 146–320), intelligence, once measured, did not change over the course of a lifetime. It was an inherited and unchangeable trait; teaching and learning had nothing to do with it.

In its original form, the IQ test was a device for diagnosing the thinking problems of people who were clearly having trouble. It was used in clinics and administered orally one-to-one. Then this clinical device became a paper-and-pencil test and was given to thousands, first in the military and later in schools, where virtually every child was tested. At some point, the testers decided to change the way they reported the results. The original measurement device was a series of little tests that were intended to explore a variety of thinking responses. But the testers began to total the scores and refer to IQ as a single score. Consequently, IQ came to be regarded as a single capacity.

Once that happened, it was easy to compare individuals. From the 1920s through the 1950s, testing enthusiasts gathered impressive statistics from paper-and-pencil IQ tests to show the superior intelligence of whites over blacks, men over women, rich over poor, Northern European over Mediterranean ancestry, and Americans of long standing over recent immigrants. Members of the so-called inferior groups composed music, acquired and ran businesses, and raised housefuls of bright, articulate children, but still the school's definition of intelligence went unquestioned.

Indeed, because IQ was supposedly unaffected by teaching and not discoverable from good performance, evidence of intelligent *behavior* was regarded as irrelevant to the meaning of the concept. The linking of intelligence with IQ tests resisted criticism. Insipid thinking by those with high IQs was (and still is) explained as intelligence not applied. Conversely, the consistently productive person could sometimes be heard laughing apologetically, "I'm an overachiever," as though their performance were deceptive when placed next to the real indicator of their ability—their IQ. Educators still tend to accept the notion of intelligence as an inner, unchangeable, unteachable, singular essence that cannot be shown except on tests.

Suzanne   Today's word *smart* is too close for comfort to *high IQ*. It's a label that sticks. Because it sticks, it marks people off into groups whose membership stays the same, sometimes for life. Suzie's mention of the way IQ was linked with ethnicity reminded me of the way "the smart ones" have been brought together by schools year after year. The same goes for the "not smart," "the remedial," "the Redbirds"— call them what you will—who have been placed side by side in one circle after another. My friend Marilyn Woods, who teaches fifth grade at Monte Vista, says that kids are never fooled. She had all her reading groups invent their own group names one year, but the children had the ranking figured out in a minute. So well did they understand who was smart and who was not that they had to only look around the small-group circle and see who was there to know who they were.

School traditions are deeply entrenched. Ability grouping is now disapproved of by California state guidelines, but schools continue the practice under the guise of "enrichment." One program in California, Gifted And Talented Education (GATE), provides extra monies for an enriched curriculum for the children who qualify. To qualify, they have to be nominated either by their parents or a teacher. But the main requirement is to do well on a battery of standardized tests. There are quotas. If more than a certain percentage meet the criteria for GATE, then the criteria are changed to ensure that no more than the set percentage are admitted.

On Tuesdays in our district, all the fifth graders in GATE are bussed to a separate school. They enjoy going. They see other friends, classes are small and the rooms uncrowded. Little homework is assigned, the curriculum is interesting, and a lot of time is available for discussion. The GATE children (and their parents) know that they are the "gifted" ones; talent—artistic talent, for example—isn't given much priority in the selection procedure.

By publicly labelling these children as the smart ones, school officials also label the ones who stay behind: the "nongifted," the "less smart." It's a sobering thought for ten-year-olds that they're considered incapable of benefitting from the mysterious things the gifted children do at GATE. Children who are nominated for GATE but don't do well enough on the battery of tests are called "average" or "limited" in the letter that goes home to the parents. I've seen children devastated by this try-and-fail procedure.

Suzie   I had my own story about ability grouping.

I once led a freshman composition program at the University of California, San Diego, called "Subject A"; students assigned to this program were termed "remedial." The course title, Subject A, effectively set these students apart from the "regulars." The program was something they had to get through before they could proceed to credit-granting university courses. It created an underclass of students.

Yet these were students from California who had graduated in the top 15 percent of their high school classes; the university didn't accept students below this line. Having taught in a California high school, I was familiar with the range of their abilities and knew what they'd been taught. When they reached the university, they needed instruction in the university's language, which was understandably strange to them, but they weren't uneducated and they weren't "remedial."

I argued with the university administrators. These students were not boneheads, I said, nor were they in need of remediation. Only the university's policy made them seem so. The time was the early 1970s, the place a campus made sensitive to issues of race and class by the presence of Herbert Marcuse and Angela Davis. It wasn't hard to persuade the faculty administrators to change the name of the course to "Lit 10," thereby allowing students to earn credit, the standard currency of the university system. This was many years ago, however. The policy and the names at San Diego have been reversed again. The old remedial status and the old course name, Subject A, are back in place.

Suzanne   It's difficult to separate a class of fifth graders into ability groups. Look at my children. There's Andrea, a whiz at spelling but scared of math. Angelo's not a quick reader—his comprehension scores are just at grade level—but he's fascinated with planets and can tell you more than you want to know about them. Marisol can read and write Spanish; Juan cannot. Daniel senses other people's feelings; Timmy doesn't. But Timmy can sing and Daniel can't carry a tune.

One whole group of children, the descendants of Sicilian fishermen who brought their boats and their families to fish in Monterey Bay a few generations ago, know about the need to negotiate to be able to work as a family unit. On the basis of which ability would I group these children?

Children are members of groups of many kinds—nuclear families, extended families, Mom's new family, Dad's new family, and peer groups in the streets, the neighborhoods, the condominium, and so on. It makes sense that in school, too, they would fall into different groups at different times of the day. They shouldn't always find themselves with the same people. One thing I do when I plan the school day is to make sure that each child is a member of several groups.

The group my children seem to like most is their "team" (which we say more about in Chapter 11). On the first day of school, the ones whose older siblings I have taught gravitate to the display of posters made by teams in past years. Each year, when the posters are finished, I get out the stepladder and stick the new ones high on the wall above the chalkboard.

Today Lori points upward. "That was my brother's team last year. The Surfer Dudes." The children laugh. The notion of Lori's brother as either a surfer or a dude is suspect. A short, chubby, pale boy, he was known for Nintendo expertise. But Surfer Dudes was the name the team members had given themselves and the name they were called by the other children.

It's clear that these invented names are loaded with intentions. How did the members of the group GLUE know that they would have such a hard time working together? The whole class laughed when the group members announced their choice of names. Even their poster—which consisted of a drawing of a container of glue, drips and dots covered with metallic glitter, and their names stuck on randomly—didn't alert me to the fact that they *knew* I had not chosen the members of this team wisely. Each member felt, deep down, that glue was needed to keep them in their chairs and their attention fixed to the matter at hand. Whoever suggested the name GLUE struck responsive chords. Group members, having publicly announced their need, tried to stick together. Sometimes they succeeded.

Another team, the Teacher Tortchers, was issuing a challenge. I wasn't to expect these children to be good little boys and girls. They were growing up, spreading their wings, taking charge. I was forewarned. I told them they had to spell Teacher Torturers correctly on the poster they were making, but I encouraged their independence. I never felt tortured, but I didn't tell them that.

The A team was making another statement. Only one member had been an *A* student before; the rest imagined that with her on their team anything was possible. They frequently gave themselves "high fives" and kept a cheerleading atmosphere buzzing at their desks.

Lori and her group will make a name for themselves and a poster too, though not Surfer Dudes, Corn Nuts, Tornadoes, or Fabulous Five, since these names have been used before. By the time her team reaches the end of the semester, they will have forged a group identity that stems from an association of ten-year-olds with differing kinds of abilities and limitations. I ensure a mix by picking the groups myself. Except for GLUE, whose members were too much alike, I generally succeed. Above all, no group is the "smart" group.

Suzie   It seemed to me, as we talked, that Suzanne was struggling against old words, having her children invent new words to create school as an invigorating place for themselves. Fortunately, though the word *smart* is colored by the school culture and by the meaning of exclusivity, *intelligence* is a word the children have seldom encountered in school. As though intelligence is a room she wants them to explore, Suzanne opens the door, saying "Come on in. You're not trespassing."

Suzanne   Each year I begin by asking the children to consider the word *intelligent* and what it means. I have in mind a definition similar to the one espoused by Howard Gardner in *Frames of Mind* (1983). Intelligence, says Gardner, is not singular; it's multiple. Part but not the whole of intelligence is verbal ability. Other parts include being musical, being skilled at figuring out human problems, and being good at observing, spatial relations, social relationships, and using memory to advantage. I like the fact that these are active rather than static qualities. They're things you *do*. They are performance and behavior.

Intelligence is not just changeable and teachable. It's a "doing" thing. It's not singular or even double; it's multiple. At least half of the children who enter into my classroom need to be shown that intelligence is within their grasp. The notion of intelligence as a doing thing empowers them to exercise control over it. They become intelligent by taking action.

If children see that mental life can be separated into different kinds of "doing" or "happening," they'll be more inclined to respect the abilities of other children. They'll see that not everyone has the same kind of smarts. They'll be more inclined to respect their own abilities too, and to adopt a swapping mentality: "I'll swap some of my kind of smarts for some of yours"—that kind of thing.

That's why I told Suzie we have to talk about the words *smart, clever,* and *intelligent* right at the beginning of the year.

On the first day or two of school I get the children to define what they're about in the fifth grade. I talk to them about "work." I work, I say, their parents work, some of their brothers and sisters work, and so on. I tell them that their work is school, and what they're doing in school is learning how to think. As we begin to talk about thinking, I ask them to make distinctions.

I say that we'll spend the year learning how to be smart, clever, and intelligent. Then we talk about the meanings of these words.

Smart means that you know the answers to 7 x 9 and the names of the continents. It's smart to know them because you're going to be asked about them again and again and you don't have to keep looking them up in books. So being *smart* is knowing the answers in school.

Clever means getting along well in the world. The children say it's knowing how to ride the bus—how to have the right change and get off at the right stop. They'll say it's clever being able to persuade people to do things and to get away with stuff. I'll say it's clever to remember Thursday night to put your homework where you can remember it on Friday morning, and it's clever to have your desk arranged so you can find things.

Clever is a difficult word, I tell them. I don't intend it to mean "devious," "cunning," or "sly," like Fagin's band of pickpockets. But I don't want to use the word *skillful* because "skills" are something that most children connect only with school, such as "math skills" or "reading skills." In a separate category between the words *smart* and *intelligent*, *clever* is the most evocative of everyday reasoning.

But being "intelligent" requires a different kind of thinking. Being intelligent is figuring out things, and in the process, wondering, puzzling, and planning. The children give the word a slightly mysterious cast. They'll say you're intelligent when you think of what's going to become of you in the future. Or come up with things that nobody has thought about before. Or invent things. Once in a while we'll all decide that it's intelligent to understand why it's helpful to be smart.

We talk about the fact that everybody—*everybody*—is able to do, more or less, some of all of these things, including mentally handicapped people as well as everybody else.

The children understand that there's more to life than being smart. Some of them have had the experience of feeling intelligent and going through the mental states of wondering and puzzling. For others there's a whole new "ahhh!", especially for those who are not smart—or do not see themselves as smart—and whose self-worth is connected with whether or not they are smart. They jump on this and think, "Ah! I see that! Maybe I'm intelligent!"

Sometimes, if we've learned something, I'll ask, "Are we being smart, clever, or intelligent?"

"Smart," someone will say. "Boy, am I smart!"

Or, if we have a hard problem to solve, I'll say, "Are we intelligent!"

Fight fire with fire, I say. In the past, schools have damaged children's sense of self by using language and grouping in well-meaning but often destructive ways. In the present, we can repair some of this damage by using language and grouping again, this time to build a different self.

The self I have in mind is a thinker. I teach the children to call themselves thinkers, and then I take it from there by asking them to consider what thinkers do.

TWO

Thinkers Ask Questions

Suzanne   Thinkers, I tell the children, ask questions. At ages ten and eleven, children are right on the edge of asking intelligent questions. This is how they differ from children five to eight, who are so filled with questions that they're not even sure what a question is. The younger children, for example, go to the assembly at the beginning of the year when a police officer comes to explain safety in the street. He tells them about crossing in the pedestrian walkway and so forth, then asks, "Are there any questions?" A child in the audience will say, "Yes, I have a question. Well, I wanted to cross the street once and I got hit by a car." The police officer will get this perplexed look on his face. Then he'll say, "That's very interesting. Are there any other . . . Are there any questions?"

"Well, my grandmother, when she . . ."

They have no questions. A child might ask, "Why do you wear handcuffs?" which is a question, but has nothing to do with what the police officer has been talking about. They don't realize that when he was talking, they should've been thinking to themselves, "I wonder why . . . I wonder if . . . I wonder what such-and-such means." Instead, they're just taking in his language and going "ohhh."

Even with ten-year-olds, asking good questions is something I have to keep talking about. "Good questions," I say, "are those that elicit an intelligent response." When someone asks one of these, I make it a point to notice. For example, if we're talking about the explorers and someone asks, "Why did they die of scurvy? Why didn't they just take orange juice or vitamin C pills?" then I'll say, "Now that's a good question." And I repeat it. Or I will ask myself questions. "Well, now, why did the Native Americans come across that land bridge? There's a good question." That way they get the idea first, that it's a question and second, that it's a good question because we really have to think about the answer.

Someone might ask, "When is it time for recess?" and I'll say, "Well, that's a question. It's not a *good* question, but I'll answer that question."

As we're learning something, I might say, "If I was making up a test about this, what kind of questions would I ask?" And somebody will say, "What were the names of Columbus' ships?" I'll say, "I don't think I'd ask that."

"Why not?"

"Because you'd all get it, you're so smart! I'm going to need an intelligent question." When this happens, there's a great pause while they all sit there and look at me with their eyes fixed and wait for somebody to do something. And usually it's Paolo, because Paolo wants to step in and be the star and everybody will go, "ooh, oooh, good, good!" It's true that Paolo asks wonderful questions. He will say something like, "Why did Queen Isabella give Columbus the money?" Then I'll ask the class, "Is that a good question?" And the children will say, "Yep." Or someone will say, "How many sails on

Columbus' ship?" And I'll ask, "Will that question get you an *intelligent* answer?"

Children are not used to the idea that questions are theirs. They're used to asking permission and asking *for* things, but asking questions such as Paolo's is something they don't do easily.

Suzie   One of the oddest things about school, Suzanne and I thought, is that children's questions are not encouraged. Textbooks ask questions at the ends of chapters, and teachers ask questions, though often as a surrogate for the textbook. But children rarely ask their own questions, and rarely do teachers ask, "What are you curious about?" By the time the teacher asks, "Are there any questions?" the children know the lesson is coming to an end. Any questions they might ask at this point are for clarification, not to satisfy curiosity.

The classroom is a small culture complete with roles and expectations. Question asking in this culture is assigned not to the learner but to the teacher, especially when the class is in the middle of a "lesson." Within the context of the lesson is "recitation," an ancient and honored practice that requires that children show what they have learned. The children's answers work like tests to assure the teacher that understanding has occurred. Questions in this context are opposite to those in the world outside of school since they are asked by someone who doesn't need the answer.

So standard is the typical teacher-as-questioner pattern that classroom researchers now refer to it as IRE: initiation, response, and evaluation. The teacher initiates with a question, the child responds, and the teacher evaluates. Harvard University researcher Courtney Cazden, who volunteered to step in as teacher so that her teacher language could be studied, found that she used the IRE sequence herself. For example, consider the transcript of a lesson on map skills, which she taught by getting the children to show on the map where their parents had come from (1988, 35).

"Who came farther, your mother from Arkansas to San Diego or your father from Baltimore to San Diego?" she asked.

"My father," the child responded.

"Yes, he came a long way," replied Cazden, evaluating the child's remark.

Within the three-part sequence, the teacher plays two roles: initiating (by asking the question) and evaluating (by saying yes). The child's rather limited role is to respond. The teacher, by initiating, sets the direction of the discourse for each sequence and by evaluating, brings the sequence to a close. The child does neither of these.

What happens, then, when children pose their own questions? They "initiate," running a certain social risk by taking momentary control of the lesson. Cazden found, when she examined the transcripts of her lessons, a rare instance during her map lesson when a child named Carolyn initiated by asking a question.

"Where's that at?" asked Carolyn, when the word *Baltimore* came up. At the time, Cazden recognized the question as helpful to both Carolyn and the class. Like Suzanne, she called attention to it: "Now *where's that at?*" she repeated. "That's a good question, Carolyn." Later, she concluded from the transcripts that the child had had to be unusually quick-tongued to have entered into the dialogue. For Carolyn to be socially appropriate, which she was, she had to be relevant, brief, and interesting. She couldn't steal the limelight from the teacher. Children asking their own questions in the middle of a lesson walk a tightrope; they risk being too long, being off the point, or being sassy.

I've noticed that callers to talk radio programs have similar problems trying to state their questions. They, too, have to be relevant, brief, and interesting. Some get bogged down in the details of their story until the host interrupts, sometimes pleading, "But what is your question?" The demand for brevity is hard to meet. People want to tell the stories behind their questions before asking the questions themselves.

Suzanne   Why do people ask questions in the first place?

Talking to Suzie about IRE, I thought about Carolyn's question "Where's that at?" This was a *real* question. It belonged to Carolyn in a way that Paolo's question "Why did Isabella lend Columbus the money?" did not. Paolo's question was offered in the spirit of trying to help the class define a *good* question. Whether it was a *real* question I couldn't be sure because I wasn't sure whether Paolo was curious about this or not. There is a difference. Often questions in the social studies textbook are good because they are near the top of Bloom's taxonomy (1956); they are intended to elicit evaluation and discussion. But usually they aren't real: The children have no reason of their own to ask them. They feel no ownership, no personal stake in the question.

"Good question" is a concept I teach. When the children interview each other at the beginning of the year, I'll say, "You might ask the other person, 'What is your favorite color?' and you'll get maybe the answer *pink*. But is *pink* something that interests you and makes you want to talk longer? Probably not. A good question interests the person you're talking to; it leads to more talk."

"But real questions are elusive," I thought to myself. "They are harder for both child and teacher to ask." As Suzie and I talked, I was struck by the way the words *children* and *teacher* could be interchanged. Could it be that teachers also are filled with questions but don't ask them because they don't know that the search to find answers is theirs? Is it possible that they, too, ask no real questions? In merely posing such a question, was I upsetting tradition? Was I suggesting that teachers, like children, are only used to asking permission and asking *for* things?

I realized I did mean this, and I do suggest this. For many years in my life as a teacher, my real questions were not encouraged. I was just a conduit through which flowed the wisdom of those who knew better. The place for questions was at the end of each chapter. They were to be answered in complete sentences and corrected with the publisher's key. Yet I was acknowledged to be a good teacher, respected by my administrators and peers, and fitting established ideas of how school runs, how teachers are, and how students learn.

Now I know that if I had asked my own questions all along, trusting my experience, I might have learned more quickly how to create the kind of community I wanted in my classroom. Earlier in my teaching life I would have asked myself, "Don't learners have to make noise?" For many years, I taught without questioning the "truth" that classrooms are quiet places, even though I knew intuitively that silence is not golden, and knew this with unshakable certainty. "Embroider that on a tea towel," I told myself: **S I L E N C E I S   N O T   G O L D E N .**

Maybe I had to have four children of my own (four in four years) to understand the value of noise, but at any rate I did learn this lesson while I was still at home with small children. I knew early in my teaching career that children get ideas more quickly when they explain them to others and when, in asking others for help, they put their problems into words. But it wasn't until 1977, when my youngest child was fourteen, that I began to see how child-to-child talk could be woven into the curriculum.

In the summer of that year, I went off to spend five weeks at the Central California Writing Project at the University of California, Santa Cruz. Lured by the prospect of peace and quiet amid the redwood trees, a pleasant break from the teen-age clamor at home, I expected yet another static professional development activity. Instead I found a powerful model of "teacher as learner."

The teacher-participants in this institute didn't sit facing the front of the room, pens poised to record someone else's wisdom. We faced each other. We were assumed to be wise—to have learned something from our experience as teachers and as people who had lived lives. We could learn from each other.

We all had questions about our own writing and learning. These questions rippled into new areas of concern, then finally made their way into old notions of who we were and what we thought we were doing. I remember John Wilkes, a University of California faculty member, describing his writing assignments for university students in a science course; he had changed his relationship with his students by beginning with their questions, which he discovered by reading their writing. He began, he said, with the students' need to know.

I left the writing project euphoric yet apprehensive. Could children in elementary school show their need to know by asking questions? And what if I kept asking my own questions? Could *my* need to know lead me to question areas of curriculum long construed by the educational hierarchy as none of my business? Could curiosity kill this cat?

That fall, I came back to teach a grade two–three classroom. As things turned out, students took enthusiastically to the new ways of writing that I had brought back with me. But my second and third graders were different from me in one way. When I tried to show them how to write in response to their own questions, they didn't seem as excited as I had been. Their public questions remained either functional—"What's for lunch today?"—or rather dull and unrelated to their real lives. I could turn their questions back to the class and ask, "What do you think about that?" but questions always seemed to revolve around my position as authority, as knower of the right answer. Both the children and I were caught in the grip of IRE. I initiated and evaluated: all that was left for them was to respond.

Later in the spring, I temporarily found a way out of IRE by taking advantage of the arrival of Henry and Mabel on their annual migration. The custodian, remembering other years when these two ducks stopped in for a week or so at nearby Lake El Estero, had a supply of bread crusts waiting on the playground. Having watched the ducks before school, both the second and third graders set to work making pictures and writing stories about Henry and Mabel.

The moment of real change in the children's questions arose when they looked at each other's drawings. Some of the ducks pictured by the second graders had four legs or paws. Could ducks have paws? The third graders thought this was funny, but their questions were serious. What *did* ducks' feet look like? Why was Mabel a different color from Henry? What made the feathers on his neck shine? Where did they come from? Where were they going? Were ducks birds?

These were questions that came from a need to know. I had previously found report writing to be passive, dreary regurgitation. Writing as part of a genuine investigation offered new possibilities. That year the children wrote about birds. They found different species to learn about, then compared and contrasted their information with that of classmates. The project was full of energy. As for me, I was learning that children asked real questions when they looked back on something they had been engaged in earlier. In this situation, it was the children who owned the questions.

Another project, this one on endangered species, brought the point home again. We started along the old, predictable path, studying my posters, my ideas, my information, and my dittos. We all liked animals and agreed it was a good idea not to be extinct, but the lesson still put me at the center of question asking. Then a pause in the teaching allowed just enough room for a child's chance remark about mammals being warm-blooded. It was an electric moment.

"You mean blood can be warm or cold?"

"*Killers* have cold blood."

"What about endangered species?"

Real questions led to more real questions. Were endangered species dangerous? What species were dangerous? What should we watch out for on a walk through the woods? Something different was happening. The difference was that this time I recognized the tone of reflection or puzzlement when I heard it. I stepped back and I waited. I gave space for the questions that finally came forth.

By this time I was moving faster in making discoveries, partly by taking my own questions seriously. I had concluded that the children had real questions, and I simply had to listen better and to give their voices more space within the framework of the lesson. I also had to make children conscious of themselves as question askers, which I could do by having children help each other construct questions.

As for my own consciousness, I remembered to give the children time. After the year of the endangered species project, I always did an investigative project, but I began to wait for the children to choose the topic. I knew that if I waited, one child would raise a question that would catch the interest of the others. Once this question came up and was recognized—one year, for example, it was "How do birds' wings work?"—then the spirit of curiosity would pass from one child to another.

The year of the question about birds' wings was the year that filmmakers came to my classroom to film a unit on how I taught writing, which would be distributed to teachers nationwide via the National Writing Project. Scheduling turned into a problem, I remember, because every time Fred Grossberg, the producer, asked me when they could come, I'd say, "The children haven't asked their real question yet. We have to wait." Fred was nervous, but of course the question finally came. In the end, the film, entitled *Flight*, showed how each child chose a question related to flying, asked more and more questions about this one question, then answered those questions by reading and writing.

That year I was puzzling over another of my own questions. How could I move beyond the boundaries of these research projects? Now that Henry and Mabel had flown away and all dangerous animals were removed, now that I had finished with investigation, I was back again in the position of chief questioner. I realized that the children no longer saw themselves as question askers. How could I make their questions a more central part of their learning in every part of the curriculum?

Sometimes I have to be hit over the head. The answer to my question came to me from the finished film *Flight*, which showed that real questions arose when the children worked with each other *in my absence*.

At that point in my teaching I was still sitting in on all small-group meetings, including the groups in which the children read their writing to one another. The funny thing was that I would have sat in with the writing groups that year too, but I had changed things when the camera crew arrived. The crew members covered up the windows and brought in artificial lighting; they moved tables and put microphones everywhere. I had to change the whole schedule. The kids, thank heavens, acted as if this all happened every week, while I just rolled with the punches. So when the cameramen wanted to film one group when I was busy with another, I said, "Go ahead and meet without me," thinking little about the result.

But the result was there in the film for anyone to see, and still is. When I saw it, I said to myself, *"The group didn't need me."* The group members' willingness to ask questions—their ownership of the situation—was just what I'd been trying to foster. But in the group I joined, I did most of the talking. I was "leader." Questions from the children were filtered through me. I restated their words. I was the teacher, doing teacherly things, however nicely or engagingly. I decided that the next year, the children would run their own groups.

The year after that, 1982, I met Suzie, whose barrage of questions raised my consciousness. By that point it was obvious to me that I, like the children, and like Suzie, was a person searching for answers. And *re*searching. As a researcher, I undertook a tape-recording project. I had my children tape their small groups so that I could hear how they were getting on. I listened carefully to the children's tapes, paying special heed to evidence that the children's question asking and commenting were improving. Then, back in the classroom, I applied what I had learned, making changes or repeating a routine where needed.

The next year, while attending the conference of the National Council of Teachers of English in Denver, I walked into a session called the "roundtable on research," where, true to the billing, the room was set with round tables at which people could talk about their experiences. It took the others at my table only a moment to discover that a teacher was in their midst—only "teacher" wasn't their name for me. "Oh, a practitioner!" said one, to which the others nodded. They made me welcome, but it was clear that they hadn't expected one of my kind to show up. Practitioners were meant to be recipients not makers of research. Practitioners and researchers didn't usually sit at the same table.

Yet I knew who I was: I was a teacher *and* a researcher. By this time Suzie and I were a research team, though *team* is probably the wrong word. We were more like cooks in the kitchen, stirring the pots as we conversed. Gradually, other cooks joined in. I often talked at length with Marilyn Woods, the other fifth-grade teacher at Monte Vista, who said to me, "Suzanne, I'd like to do some of the things you're doing." That was all the encouragement I needed. From that day on, Marilyn helped me figure out what research questions we were asking. Then, when Suzie arrived in the summer, those questions became the topics of our conversations, which Marilyn became a part of.

Suzie's questions were always a little different from Marilyn's and mine. She had a slightly different perspective, as though she were outside looking in. That's why her questions were stimulating. At the same time, she made me see that our questions, though different from hers, were important.

Suzie and I have quite a different relationship from other teacher/researcher teams. Often such pairs consist of a secondary or elementary school teacher *and* a university-based researcher rather than two teachers *as* researchers. When university graduate students go into classrooms to conduct ethnographic research, for example, the teacher is not a researcher. The teacher and the classroom provide the data for study, and the university person interprets. In our case, I'm both teacher and researcher. Suzie, a university faculty member, is a fellow researcher; she listens, talks, and looks at my collected materials with me. But only rarely, because of our teaching schedules and the difficulty of travel, does she sit in my classroom. I'm not the subject of her research. Both of us write, and both of us interpret.

Suzie   Traditionally, teachers of grades K-12 are not researchers. Research takes time, and teachers are not paid to spend their time asking questions and doing all the data collection and writing that research requires. Consequently, research typically is done by university people, whose schedules allow for it and whose promotion and tenure demand it. These people, it turns out, formulate the questions that become the established questions for doing research within their academic communities. So research questions about schools and teaching are generally formulated by academics rather than teachers.

I found, when I began directing the Subject A writing program in San Diego in the early seventies, that the established set of educational research questions did not apply. I did not want to ask "Which of two different methods, experimental or control, gives better results?" I had only one method and I did not want to set up a different one merely for purposes of a study. I wanted to study what was in front of me, the ongoing interaction between tutor and freshman. What went on between them in the process of going over the draft of an essay, and how might that conversation lead to discovery and to changes in the draft? I wanted to know.

Fortunately, it had become easier in the early seventies for writing teachers to convert such questions into research questions. Janet Emig's well-known study of student composing (1971) had departed from the standard "Which of two methods?" question. Working in the San Diego program, I began to realize how many real questions I had about student writers.

I discovered these questions when I conversed every day for at least half an hour with my coworker Adela Karliner. Both Adela and I taught sections of writing, incorporating the work of tutors in a workshop setting, rather like a studio art class. Both of us also worked one-to-one with students who saw us on an appointment basis about writing course papers. Both of us had small children whose language and social development fascinated us. We became curious to know more about the language of our classroom—the language of brainstorming, of critique, of analysis—that we could hear only in tantalizing fragments. The tape recorder became a tool. With it we could replay that language and reflect on its effectiveness as a tool for thought.

This entire set of circumstances—the collaborative relationship with another teacher, the more accommodating research methodologies, the time we had for conversation, and the tape recorder—made it possible for the two of us to be teacher-researchers. Encouraged as well by the efforts of James Britton, Nancy Martin, and others, whose cooperative research with teachers at the University of London and whose interest in classroom language were now well known in the United States (1975), we set to work transcribing tapes. In the end, Adela and I found ourselves with more questions (Jacobs and Karliner 1977). Why was it that some students entered into the spirit of conversational exchange, supporting the thought processes of their partners, but other students dominated the conversation? What was the ideal supporting role in these exchanges? How could we teach this role? Could the dominating student be led to change?

In 1982, when I met Suzanne on Maui, not only did I still relish the thought of doing collaborative research with another teacher, but I was also still mulling over these questions about the effectiveness of students helping students. That's why I was so interested in Suzanne's small groups.

"Can ten-year-olds handle the responsibility?" I asked her. Even at the college level, students couldn't always help each other effectively. Could ten-year-olds carry off group meetings without a teacher sitting in?

"Not always," she said. It was an old question: how could children learn how to think independently if the teacher always guided them, yet how could they practice guiding themselves in small-group meetings if they were socially immature?

Over the years, from the time of our first meeting in 1982 right up to the time of writing this book, I have asked Suzanne this question every once in a while, and over the years Suzanne has conceded the difficulties. She has told me her stories of what teachers euphemistically call "problems": the children who sabotage the group effort if they can't always be leader, the gigglers with two-minute attention spans. Even the well-behaved can wander away from the task at hand.

Elizabeth Cohen, a sociologist from Stanford who has studied the dynamics of teacherless groups (1986, 20–33), says that children's classroom groups can fall apart in at least two ways. In her view, these problems are caused by gaps in status. High-status children, the ones who are usually at the top of the class, can dominate the group so completely that the assigned job gets finished before the other members have a chance to participate. That's one kind of failure. Or groups without recognized leaders may simply flounder and never get the job done. Members of these groups get completely off track and chat about something else (Suzanne calls this "recess talk"), or push their chairs aside so as not to form a group at all. This is a second kind of failure. To avoid both, says Cohen, groups need to have a strong sense of purpose and a clear idea of exactly what to do.

"How do you tell the children exactly what to do?" I asked Suzanne.

"I don't," she said.

I had doubts. When the teacher asks children to conduct small groups on their own, she asks them to change all the traditional social roles. Who will initiate if the teacher is absent? Will the children use a question-and-answer pattern of talk? Will they model their exchanges after IRE, one of them playing the role of teacher? If not the IRE pattern, then what pattern of talk will they use, and where will they see this pattern demonstrated?

"Don't you have to teach them what to say to one another in the group?"

"No," said Suzanne, "I never tell the children what to say in a group. Figuring out what to say is part of the way they form a relationship with each other; it's part of their power."

"But you're the teacher," I said, "and you teach them basically how to talk in the group."

"No," she insisted. "I don't."

Suzanne   Suzie brought up questions of culture. "Do you see a cultural pattern in the group behavior?" she asked me.

"Oh, yes, certainly," I answered. "They've learned in school that the questions don't really belong to them. This is part of the school culture."

But Suzie was talking about culture in the home and ethnicity. My school, a public school, invites a mix of nationalities and home cultures. Anyone on the block can come. Won't schools in Japan—where culture is homogeneous—have an easier time teaching group behavior? Suzie wondered. She knew that I had gone to a parochial school until I was nine years old. Wouldn't the nuns in my old school have had an easier time of it than I was having? She wondered if the cultural mix in the classroom didn't make group work hard to handle.

"Not really," I thought.

There are two kinds of culture: ethnic culture, which comes from home, and the culture of the school. Each plays its part. I've had girls come into my class from the Middle East. A Turkish girl, I remember, was very quiet; her father said to me at the parent conference, "Girls in our culture are not outspoken." And Japanese-American children, for all their variousness, I still find to be less inclined to speak up in class than Caucasian children. The home culture teaches some children to be quiet until they are certain they know the answers and to be wary of looking ignorant, which they might if they ask their questions aloud.

But the school culture plays an even bigger part. All children, no matter where they come from, have learned to play their roles in the IRE routine. Their ethnic differences look pale next to their sameness in the way they behave in the classroom. They've all learned the same school culture, and they all have to unlearn some of that when they start working in teacherless groups.

As I told Suzie, about some things I felt unshakably certain. Ten-year-olds are often socially immature. It is also a given that, in California, children are culturally diverse; some of their home cultures are far different from the culture of school. A third given is that children should work without the teacher in small groups for at least part of the day. I knew this in my bones.

But still puzzling me was how, in the face of these three givens, a teacher can teach children to be askers of real questions, to be really curious. How are good questions and real questions different? Can't a question be both? Of course. So what is the role of the teacher? The role of the teacher is to see that the questions asked are both real and good, isn't it? And how does the teacher do this? In the case of the ducks' paws question, the teacher did two things: (1) established an atmosphere where real questions could arise, and (2) established an atmosphere where the real could be transformed into the good. Maybe the teacher also did a third thing: made sure that the "real" in the question stayed there and didn't get removed during the process of making it good.

Still, "establishing an atmosphere" was a vague idea. How was I to do this? I was sure I didn't tell children what to say to one another in the groups, but how did I show them a role that was different from the role dictated by IRE? These questions were not just academic. Both Marilyn and I by this time were giving workshops to other teachers as well as teaching a night class to teachers in training. I needed the answers for these teachers, not to mention Suzie, who kept calling from Honolulu. She didn't let up and neither did I.

THREE

The Social Side of the Brain

Suzie This chapter takes us back to "intelligence" and the idea of the swapping mentality mentioned in chapter 1. "I'll swap some of my smarts for some of yours—that sort of thing." At the top of the list are "how" questions: how does a teacher create a classroom culture, or atmosphere, that cultivates this mentality? Our answer, which is elaborated in the rest of this book, is that a teacher creates a consciousness of social responsibility. Children have responsibilities for the well-being of the other children in the class. In this chapter we give the word *thinker* a social meaning, thus the chapter title "The Social Side of the Brain."

Suzanne

••••••••••
This chapter also takes us back to groups and the question of how to teach ten-year-olds what to do without a teacher sitting in.

I've used group work in my teaching almost from the start and have learned from experience that setting children face-to-face and knee-to-knee almost always leads to interaction but not necessarily to helpful collaboration. I've had children like Casey, who was so eager to help the others that she figured she could be substitute teacher if I was ever sick. But I've also had "Charles the ghost." Not only did Charles never speak, but when his groups met, he'd push his chair back until they got the message he wasn't there. When it was his turn to chair the team, he could never remember what to do. The rest of the team had to tell him. When he entered the class, his reading scores were actually years below grade level, though he had no learning disability nor did he come from a troubled family. He looked sleepy most of the time, and occasionally surprised, as though startled at not being home watching television. He stared off into the distance or ambled to the water fountain for drinks. Whenever his group worked on a problem, he'd fold his arms and lean back.

Gradually, Charles began to tune in because so many demands were being made of him by other children. "What'd you get for number six?" they'd ask. They needed his answer because they couldn't write their math work into their learning logs until they could say whether their answers agreed with the other answers at their table. When he was chairperson of his team, a person who had been absent might ask, "Where are the assignments from yesterday?" and be annoyed when he didn't have them. He finally got tired of the children being so exasperated with him. First one way and then another he began to listen. Fortunately, they liked him and he knew it, so when they began asking him all these questions, he took it in good spirit. Little by little, he woke up. He started to anticipate his turn at giving math answers, or representing his team at the blackboard. His end-of-year reading scores showed a four-year gain over the previous year. Maybe when the teacher had given the test a year earlier, Charles hadn't even tried.

Most teachers are like me. We spend way too many of our waking hours, not to mention some of our sleeping ones, rehearsing ingenious plans for dealing with the few children like Charles, who are extremes. We ought to realize there's a little bit of Charles in most children. They all need help with social skills. Few are as quick to offer help as Casey, and even Casey doesn't always know when to offer help and how to stop short of giving too much.

In my part of California, followers of Robert Slavin (1988) have been brought in by the county office of education to give workshops on how to do cooperative learning—in other words, learning in groups. These are teacherless groups. The intended message is that children really can teach other children and that teachers are not necessarily loafing if the children are doing the talking. This is all to the good.

The trouble I have with cooperative learning is its scripted, somewhat mechanical approach. A typical sequence suggested by the workshop leaders is for the children in a given group to learn something and then to split up, each child going to a different group and teaching what was learned to the members of the new group. The technique has the spirit of a game, but also, as with a game, the rules for what to do are arbitrary. I remember sitting in a cooperative learning workshop as a group member. "Time's up," the leader said. "You've done what you're supposed to do. Now join another group." What we were supposed to do was to follow a plan—a kind of script—for what we should say to one another. But sitting face-to-face with other teachers, I really had things to say that the script interfered with. I think the other teachers felt the same. As a result, the group talk was far from what any of us wanted to talk about. Our only comfort was that we had done our job.

Ten-year-olds are not that different. When they come together in a group to talk about the books they're reading or the writing they're doing, and when they've spent time on this reading or writing, they also have things they really want to say to one another.

We're talking again about real questions and a sense of ownership. When I attend these workshops I sometimes want to stand up and say, "Beware. Ownership is a fragile thing. What we're telling the children is: 'This is your group but you should ask one another my questions or the book's questions.' This seems to me the wrong way to assure children that the schoolroom learning activity belongs to them."

The worst thing about a scripted approach is that the children may actually feel as I did in the teacher workshop: "Oh, well, I've done my job." It's not a great feeling, but there's a measure of dull comfort in it. It's easy to get used to.

An alternative to giving scriptlike help is to raise children's consciousness of who they are—their identity—as they sit in the group. I tell the children from the first day that their role is to be teachers, and that they're placed in groups so that they can teach one another. "I'm waiting for a few weeks to put you in your teams," I tell them, "because I need to find out the areas where you are smart, or clever, or intelligent. Then I'll place you where you can be of help." Partly I'm telling them not to get too settled in the seats they've chosen on the first day, and partly I'm teaching them a sense of themselves as thinkers and teachers.

Over the years I've come to see that I can teach this image of the self, and that this is a teaching role underlying all my others. I work at this image building day after day.

Suzie   "The social side of the brain" is a strange metaphor only because the history of thought in Western society has made it strange. Mouths, ears, and even hands are social. But brains? Brains are intellectual. Further consideration tells us that brain power and social skill connect and overlap in several ways. We need brain power to anticipate the other person's point of view, to support another person's creative speech, to imagine what makes someone else angry, to envision ways to help, even to decide what to say by way of condolence or greeting. Good relationships in all sorts of situations—especially cross-cultural, familial, corporate, and school—require good brains. But the image of the helping, nurturing, socially responsible person stubbornly separates itself in Western culture from both "intelligence" and "intellect." Barbara Rogoff, a noted scholar of child development, cites studies of societies in Uganda, Kenya, and the Western Pacific that show that people in these cultures find it difficult to conceive of "technical intelligence" without "social re-sponsibility" (1990, 58). They assume that the two are designated by the same word.

Why should the idea of a "doing intelligence" be separate from social responsibility? In real life they are intertwined. Mary Catherine Bateson (1989) argues that the most profitable and intelligent thing a corporate executive can do is to support underling technical experts by listening to them and asking and reasking questions; by being, in other words, a supportive partner. Too often, she notes, executives demand that underlings support them in these ways, as though this support were a kind of perquisite of their position, but they don't lend their own in return. This is not, in her view, intelligent behavior.

We assume in colleges of education that teaching the "matter" of a discipline such as language arts or mathematics is somehow separate from teaching the children to work well with each other. Traditionally, "Classroom Management" is a separate course. But structures of human interaction and structures of cognition belong in the same textbook. When students of education become classroom teachers, they invariably find that nurturing the intellect requires the nurturing of child-to-child relationships.

Suzanne Every year, for two to three months, I do a unit on the brain (see Figure 3–1), which may do more than anything else to teach children to accept an image of themselves as smart, clever, and intelligent and to accept the logic that if they're any one of these, they're ready to teach someone else. I start out with the idea of brains as power and adventure; eventually, we come around to talking about the connections between ourselves and others. Social responsibility always makes its way into the discussions. It becomes part of the brain unit.

I use my health and science time for this unit, though, as I tell the children, the brain unit is pigeonholed this way only for the report card. "Actually," I say, "this unit will teach you how the whole class works."

My Brain

My cerebrum is the biggest part of my brain, and it helps me to figure out things such as math, puzzles, and spelling.

And the cerebrum helps me make decisions •Like last night I had a choice of steak or spagetti. And when I went to the fair, I decided to go in the haunted hous instead of the high slide.

FIGURE 3–1   Writing for the Brain Unit (Two Unedited Excerpts)

As I begin the unit, I tell the children that this year is an adventure, like the book, *Great Brain* (Fitzgerald 1972). I enjoy teaching, I say, because how people think and how they learn fascinate me. Adults haven't a clue about how they think. They know they do, but how it happens is a big mystery to them.

Mystery and *adventure* are the important words here. I say to the children that we now need to explore the mystery of their brains.

First I have them draw their brains to show what they're thinking. I give them a silhouette with an outline of the brain, and I talk to them about "what's on their minds."

"Right now," I say, "a number of things are going on in your head. You may know that you are holding a pencil in your hand, be conscious of your chair, and be conscious of where you are. You may know that you're in school, that the sun is shining through the windows, and whether you're hungry. Or while I'm talking, maybe you're thinking about something else, about sitting next to so-and-so. All these things are happening in your brain at the same time. When you stop to think about it, you realize this. So, on your silhouette, show in words or little picture symbols what's on *your* mind." Then they draw in these little symbols.

When they're through, we hang up the silhouettes. There'll be dollar signs and Mom—and sometimes Mom has a real angry look on her face. Or there'll be hearts with the name of a friend, or a hamburger, or homework, or a picture of a book or a pencil—all the sorts of things you'd expect children to think about. I don't say the "back" or "front" of the mind, but the immediate things make their way to the front of the brain, and "homework" or "feed the dog" will be in the back.

After the silhouettes have been up for about a week, and have been looked at and admired, we make folders and put the silhouettes on the front. Inside we keep a record of the various activities we do on the brain, including worksheets and such that I've pulled from published materials on thinking.

For example, some years I use an idea I borrowed from a "learning poster activity card" that is published by the Education Today Company, Palo Alto, CA. I have the children keep a brain journal for a week or two, or longer if they wish. "Put the dream journal under your pillow," I tell them, "and write or draw in it as soon as you wake up. Even when you are asleep, your brain works." I tell them that ideas are like seeds. You plant an idea in your brain, your brain grows the idea by dreaming, then you harvest the idea by writing, drawing, or painting. The children share the journal by reading aloud or showing their drawings.

I also have the children interview left-handed people in the class and at home, and discuss the advantages and disadvantages of being left-handed. Then we talk about how left-handedness works physiologically. The children also do experiments. For example, they investigate the movement of eyes when people are asked questions, how pupils expand and contract, how the eyes move to the left, or to the right, or stay straight.

Then we talk about the brain, based on what we know from everyday life. I always bring up the point about control—self-control—and how things that happen in the brain might make it hard for people to control what they do. We talk about Alzheimer's disease and about mental illness of all kinds. We talk about alcoholism and drugs, which the children know about and can discuss. They'll tell how someone had a tumor on the brain and they died or didn't die. They have lots of stories to tell by the time they're nine or ten years old, so I need to allow time for them to tell all the stories. Not just one story and move on. They have to tell them all.

There's also my husband's famous brain operation. Of course, Mr. Brady didn't have to have his brain operated on just for my brain unit, but it certainly helped. I talk about how his brain had been pushed in by a blood clot. I tell the children that he had seizures and what seizures are (the electrical connections of his brain were trying to get themselves sorted out and they would misfire). The children are fascinated by that, and of course they want to know if he's all right now. They're relieved to hear that he is.

The children also are interested in sleep and what happens when you dream. They're intrigued by the fact that people still are theorizing about what happens during dreaming. They sympathize with those of us whose brains don't wake up with the rest of our bodies when the alarm clock goes off in the morning.

We also talk about whether the brain has control over feelings and the fact that feelings just seem to happen. They come up from wherever they come up from and overwhelm a person. Children have commented that it must be hard for actors and actresses to cry on cue since no amount of willpower can bring forth tears if there are no reasons for them. I mention depression, how people are sad for no particular reason. I say that depression is a feeling that needs to be mentioned to somebody so that the depressed person gets help.

Then they watch parts of the "Nova" television programs, which show the growing brain in the fetus and its development through the first year of life. They see the part about the musician who loses his memory because a brain disease makes him constantly forget. They learn that he has to be reintroduced to his wife every time he sees her and that, although he writes in his journal every day, he denies having written anything because he can't remember having done it. All he can remember are songs, and all he can still do and remember doing is conduct the choir.

So we talk about how complicated the brain is, how people don't know how it works, how you dredge up things from your memory, how things get stuck in your memory, and all this in spite of the fact that brain researchers don't know yet where memory is located.

That's when I talk about memorizing, which, I tell the children, will be important to them in math, for example. They must memorize number facts as part of the minimum competency math test: one hundred math facts in five minutes. No one can use fingers since time does not allow this.

I sometimes use an example to show that memorizing is an everyday thing. "Suppose," I say to one child, "that I ask you your name and you say 'Stanley.' You don't say, 'Well, let's see, this morning when I got up, my mother said, *Stanley, you're gonna be late,* so *my name must be Stanley.*' No, you've memorized your name, and you've memorized other things. And if you must memorize, there are tricks to doing it, which we'll talk about."

That's when we talk about the meaning of *smart:* it's smart to have things in your memory because you can haul them out whenever you need them and you don't have to go through this complicated process of "Now let me see, what was it my mother called me this morning?"

The children have all sorts of things to say about tricks of memory. They'll say, "Do you know how I remember the colors of the rainbow? I remember *Roy G. Biv*" (red, orange, yellow, etc.). And they'll also have ways to remember the streets where their friends live, telephone numbers, and addresses. They don't have a language for saying "This is what I'm doing," but whenever I touch on one of these methods, some will know they've done it.

By now it's been demonstrated to the children that smart and clever overlap, since memory is useful for knowledge of the real world as well as school. More and more I want to show them that they learn both in and out of school. By being aware of themselves as thinkers, they can use cleverness—knowing how to do things in the world—to make themselves smart—that is, smart in school. As for intelligence, I'm waiting for the day when they ask me where it's located in the brain. I can tell them with complete honesty, "That's another thing I don't know. But the fact that you've asked the question is proof that intelligence is happening in your brain."

Suzie Listening to Suzanne, I remembered the Scarecrow's song from the film *The Wizard of Oz*.

> If I only had a brain,
> Only had a brain.

But Suzanne's was a song celebrating the fact that her children had brains already. What a glorious fact! Children, like author Frank Baum's Dorothy (*The Wonderful Wizard of Oz* 1986), have powerful and active brains. With brains such as these, are they not capable of helping other children?

In answer to my old question "How do you teach them what to say in the group?" Suzanne, rather than suggesting what to say, was building a social consciousness to serve as a foundation for group work. The Scarecrow was, after all, a member of a small group. The journey to the Emerald City was a group journey, and the lessons learned by Dorothy, the Tin Man, the Cowardly Lion, and the Scarecrow were gained from their adventures together. Without technological superweapons, Dorothy and her group traveled the road on a tankful of ingenuity—plus courage, of course. Didn't the Scarecrow, when he finally reached the presence of the great Oz, find that he had a brain already? As it turned out, Oz was a fraud and had no real magic. The power was in the self, a self created in the course of travels with others.

I began to think at this point about the way stories make us see connections. Just as I had built connections to the brain unit by comparing it with a story that was well known to me, the children seemed to make meaning for themselves by making connections to stories known to them. "What did you mean," I asked Suzanne, "when you said 'We have to hear all of their stories, not just some of them.' Why the emphasis on stories?"

Suzanne   Stories are important for several reasons. Stories give the children entry into the class conversation. Stories are the bridge between them and what we're doing in class. The children have to feel that we're talking about the life of each person in the class. They tell about themselves, about people they know, and about things that they've thought about. Stories are their contribution to knowledge, to the school curriculum.

As time passes, the children keep referring back to these stories because that's how they make connections. "Well, we must be talking about *this,* and she must mean *that,* and what so-and-so had to say about her uncle must mean that we're also talking about my grandmother."

Teachers often speak of the "scaffolding" that they build, meaning the structures they erect to make it easy for children to participate in a class routine. The idea of scaffolding is that the teacher is on the spot, participating in the routine so as to model what the children should do. That's what I'm doing when I tell my own stories while sitting on the rug with them. I'm indicating that story telling is a legitimate way to contribute.

Particularly memorable stories serve as points of connection with others. For example, Katie's grandfather had Alzheimer's disease for nine or ten years before he died, which was devastating for the family. It was really hard for her mother when the grandfather didn't remember her anymore. So when Katie's story led first to talk of memory and how it is that memory just *goes,* then to how people make jokes about Alzheimer's (like me when I lose my glasses and say, "Oh, it must be my Alzheimer's"), the idea of how hard it was for Katie's mother was still there with the children. They understood that people make jokes because Alzheimer's is such a scary thing, and that I, for example, really hope that my forgetting things is *not* Alzheimer's. They kept going back to Katie's story, even when we had moved on to other topics, as though they needed this story to make a connection with whatever we were then discussing.

Michaela, I remember, told a story about a man sitting on a bench and waving. "He wasn't old at all," she said. She herself was on a bus that pulled up in front of the bench. The man made no move to get on board. At first, head down, he talked to himself, then he lifted his head, smiled at the passengers, and waved. He was in the sunshine warming himself. His shoes were wrapped in duct tape. "I didn't know what to do," said Michaela. The other passengers had turned their heads away. "I smiled," she said, "but I didn't wave."

For Michaela, all this was strange. Here was a man who did none of the expected things. The fact that she remembered the duct tape on his shoes meant that she had retained a camera shot in her mind long after the incident. A common theme in many of these stories is uncertainty—sometimes mystery—and not knowing what to do or how to explain it all. And the children want to know. That's why they sit there and listen so hard.

These stories are different from talking about "Did everyone see the lightning storm last night?" and everyone waving their hands in the air to tell you about where they were when it happened, and how it affected them, and that sort of thing. When they listen to stories like Michaela's, their posture is different. They look carefully at the people who're talking. There are fairly long pauses, but no one moves. No one plays with their erasers or checks the clock to see if it's recess. The atmosphere is hard to describe, but it feels heavy with empathy. The only time these discussions stop is if a bell rings or the children have to go somewhere. Otherwise, they can sit and talk all afternoon, and sometimes they do. Something that gets said with these stories is that, as a class, we care about each other.

As the children study brains, they become deeply interested in a common mystery, develop an excited sense of the potential of their own brains, and in the end find themselves—like Michaela—instinctively wanting to wave back, or in some way make connections to the social world. The language of the classroom discussion puts the connections into words:

> I have a dynamic brain and so do you.
>
> Your story is related to mine, my uncle to your grandfather, as I am related to you and you to me.
>
> My brain puts me in control. Not everybody has the same control I do.

By the end of November we've finished most of these projects. But the children keep their brain unit folders in their desks for the occasional times when we do something that might be appropriate for this folder. Overall, the unit gives me a way to refer back to brains and thinking all year long.

Suzie   When I first began to teach high school English many years ago I saw learning as something that went on inside heads. Learners were solo, independent, and contemplative. They had to turn off the radio and shush their friends, leaving their social selves aside and turning inward to their intellectual selves. I thought that's how I myself had learned.

I was wrong. Interacting with other people was much more important to my learning than I gave it credit for. But then others were wrong as well. I was in synch with an educational establishment that saw learning in individual terms and saw competition as the only social relationship that had anything to do with learning. Individualized instruction was sold in kits and talked up in meetings as the key to motivation. I remember images of mountain climbing: students were to see themselves struggling and sweating in their effort to reach the peak. It was important to get there first.

The trouble was that individualized learning wasn't invigorating; it wasn't outdoors. Children working their way through individualized learning kits sat at desks right next to other children—potential sources of collaboration who remained silent. They were not on a mountainside, and what they were doing was very different from climbing. But these facts went unrecognized by those who published teaching materials and set goals. Teachers were encouraged to teach children rules for behavior, but little about how they would work together in a social setting.

I remember with particular horror how bored students were with the individualized reading program put out by SRA (Science Research Associates). None but the eager beavers wanted to read the skimpy passages, race through the written comprehension exercises, chart their own scores, then move upward to ever more challenging reading. The one time I tried this with junior high school readers, they sat in their seats looking tired and peeking at the clock.

Suzanne's ideas, which impressed me profoundly, had progressed far beyond the ethic of individualized achievement. Hers was not a vision of the solitary learner climbing a mountain toward a golden reward. Feeling responsive *to,* and responsible *for*—this was the ethic of her classroom.

Suzanne
I sometimes forget how necessary it is to talk with beginning teachers about the scaffolding of social skill and social responsibility. It's become second nature to me in my own teaching. But occasionally a child will enter the class late in the year from another school, which abruptly reminds me. Suzie's remarks about individual achievement bring back to mind little Brian, who had to be told, all the time, every day, exactly what to do. A capable student, he'd just moved to Monterey. But he just sat. This went on for two or three weeks while I was getting to know him, and finally I asked his mother to come in. I said, "This is not working. What is the problem?" We chatted about things, and she said, "He was one of the best students in his school, and he got all 'very goods' on his report card." I suggested that maybe it was the trauma of the move. He was just sitting there and I had to tell him everything to do.

Then I asked her what kind of class Brian had been in. Well, he had come to Monterey from a little school that spent piles of money on individualized learning. He had spent practically his entire primary-school experience working one-to-one. He couldn't think on his own. He couldn't do anything unless an adult teacher spoke directly to him, told him how to do things, and then did a few examples for him. Only then would he work. So it was hard for him to switch over to a collaborative style of learning. I said to him, "You realize that you're a smart boy and that you really can do these things. You don't need me to do two examples for you when there are other children at your table." And by the end of the year he was doing fine.

But all this was a shock to Brian's system. His previous school had crippled him academically by giving him all this individualized curriculum. He never had learned how to work with other children, nor to learn *from* them.

Suzie   Dialogue is the basic activity of group work, and it is basic to the philosophy of teaching outlined in this book. How to invite dialogue and how to make it an instrument of thinking are questions that we take up in detail in the next several chapters.

In those chapters we address the question "How do you teach them what to say in the group?" by describing the ways in which Suzanne teaches group routines. These routines are scaffolds—structures that make it easy for each child to contribute to the group effort. For each social routine the dialogue is somewhat different because of differences in subject matter: the writing response group has a dialogue style different from those of the book groups and the teams.

Dialogue differences stem from our history; they have developed out of people's conversations and ways of making knowledge in the last several hundred years. The children most likely to attract our attention as bright and verbal are those in dialogue with past tradition; they've picked up some of its dialogue routines or styles of thought, while at the same time they personally engage with these routines, even transforming them and inventing new ones as people have done throughout history.

It's easy to forget the historical and cultural dimensions of the "bright" child's ways of knowing. The knowledge invented by our forebears and passed down to us includes not only the alphabet but various other technologies that made reading and writing easier, more engaging, and accessible to large numbers of people in all sorts of adult occupations. Consider the lab report, long division, haiku poems, and the syllogism, all of them inventions of people in the past who wanted or needed them.

Our present-day dialogues, both in speech and writing, are deeply influenced by the forms of speech and writing we've inherited from our past—from preachers, song makers, poets, kings, politicians, mathematicians, and scientists. At the same time, present-day dialogues lead to the invention of new forms, parallel to the lab report and long division but different, which are passed on, in their turn, or perhaps discarded and forgotten. Can anyone predict the future of the current talk-show idiom, of advertising copy, or the sound bite?

Styles of discourse for responding to text or making a plan are known already to some ten-year-olds, but they are known to most only as fragments, just as Spanish is known by English speakers only in bits and pieces. Some children are fluent questioners because they've been in on freewheeling discussions outside of school, but many are not. Some can speak problem-solving language; others haven't a clue about how to do this.

When children have many opportunities to speak these special discourse styles with one another, they pick them up. They become more fluent. Then an interesting thing happens, something I've noticed again and again with my students: speech turns into thought. The Russian learning theorist Vygotsky describes this important phenomenon by saying: *the spoken dialogue goes inside, becoming inner conversation* (1978, 57). Vygotsky uses the term *inner speech* (mainly in Vygotsky 1962), meaning that our pondering and cogitating have roots in the language we've heard spoken aloud. The ability to think constructively in steps—in various forms of logic, or what some call critical thinking—is dialogue internalized.

Teachers know that thinking through a problem inwardly—having an inner dialogue—is difficult for beginners. Vygotsky (1978) suggests why this is so. Thinking inwardly is an end result of a learning process. Speech really occurs first in the life of the learner. Children can "think" in group-supported speech well before they can manage the same sequence in inner speech.

This chapter has developed two lines of thought. On one hand, the influence of the past is real. Cultural traditions have built a wall between social and academic intelligence, have made academic endeavor competitive rather than collaborative, and have also left us a legacy of discourse forms and knowledge. On the other hand, the challenge of the present-day classroom is that children, here "from everywhere," have varying amounts of experience with the linguistic legacy of the past, its styles of thought, and its prejudices. Even more so, they vary in their experience working with others. Vygotskian insights weave the two strands together: the legacy of cultural tradition and a theory of thinking that emphasizes collaborative interaction among children.

A classroom in which children teach each other by means of dialogue is a classroom in which children, almost without realizing it, place their own imprint on what they learn. Talking with other children requires them continually to express what they know in terms related to their prior experience. Rather than parroting the traditions of the past, they transform. Rather than climbing mountains to get to the top first, they work collaboratively, sometimes noisily, with one another.

FOUR

The Writing Response Group

Suzie   Among those dialogues that go underground in the Vygotskian sense is the dialogue that craftspeople engage in with people working in the same craft. In the case of writing, people over time have formed clubs, groups, and societies whose members discuss the progress of their work. One of the most recent of these forums is the small response group, whose members read their work in progress aloud to one another and listen to conversational response from the other members. The idea of such groups, their purpose and method, was set out clearly by Peter Elbow, a writing teacher, in his book *Writing Without Teachers* (1973). Read your work in progress, he said. Listen to yourself saying your words aloud, sit face-to-face with your readers, listen to their questions and comments. Then decide for yourself what was strong, what was working, where the readers needed more, and what was getting in the way. Then go back to your writing and revise.

Over the years of teaching in San Diego, I began to realize that writers need a social ritual that strictly lays out the rules for listening to another person's writing: rules for when to listen, how to listen, how to respond, and how to do all of this so as to help the writer. But I had no experience of sitting down and playing a listening game until I moved to Honolulu, where I joined one of the Elbow groups set up by Roger Whitlock.

Elbow groups were Roger's specialty. He set up and became a member of two or three groups himself, taught teachers in the Hawaii Writing Project how to do them, and they, in turn, taught their students. My son was a regular member of Elbow groups in his high school creative writing course, which was taught by one of the teachers taught by Roger. My son and others in that class became AWKs (Advanced Writing Kids), who were sent out to other classes in the school to demonstrate how the groups worked. A few times, he and some friends gathered on our lanai to do Elbow groups in place of the usual board games they liked to play.

My own Elbow group meeting with Roger was a not-so-gentle nudge. Each week I had to get busy and write—something, anything, any raw piece, or any revision—or I'd have nothing to share. As things turned out, I began to look forward to these meetings. The group told me surprising things.

I also liked meeting for the opposite reason: I could anticipate what would happen. The first of the four people in the group read aloud for seven minutes any piece of writing in progress. The other three listened—just listened—then jotted a quick comment. The reader read the same piece a second time, during which the other three jotted the exact words or phrases that made something happen in their minds. Then each of three responders took turns telling the writer what words they had jotted down and what the words had reminded them of, had made them think, or made them envision. In short, they told their mental experience at the moment of hearing the words. If they got lost or distracted while listening, if they lost the point, they said so. If a word felt right, they told the writer. They described their sense of the point being made, their feelings and memories evoked by the piece, their sense of the person behind the words—all the reactions experienced by readers at the point of reading. We tried to do what Elbow had advised: "Give the writer a movie of your mind."

"I like your word *feisty*," Roger would tell me. "I like the voice here."

"The first sentence came on strong," I'd say. "I liked the way it rolled forward."

"How much was he paid?" someone would say to the writer, "and where did that money come from?"

The question responses helped us enormously because they helped us understand what the reader needed to know. There were times when a simple question made me realize I should revamp the whole piece of writing. Most times, though, the questions helped me understand where the piece should go next. Like a light, they showed me the path ahead. When the writing was going nowhere, and I felt like giving up on it because there was nothing to say, a responder's question made me think, "There *is* something to say." I'd leave the group meeting knowing what it was.

Roger firmly enforced the rules in our early meetings. "No prefacing," he said, meaning that no one should be allowed to talk about their piece before reading it aloud, either to interpret it for the group or to apologize. The writer might reveal the intended audience, but otherwise no preface was permitted. If we stuck to the text alone, then we heard response to the text, and that's what we wanted. Ground rule number one was "No prefacing."

Ground rule number two was "Don't respond to the response." In other words, if a responder asked, "Where did the money come from?" I was not to launch into an answer. If Roger, as responder, showed that he had misunderstood my meaning, I was not to correct him. What I was supposed to do was to write down the question or the wrong interpretation, whatever the response was. The point of the exercise was not to set the responder straight, but rather to ask myself, later on, "Do I want to leave the words this way, or do I want to change them?"

Back home, after the group meeting, each writer was left to ponder why some whole passages evoked nothing, why some words but not others had made responders nod in agreement, or why some words had triggered the response "sounds very businesslike." Still in charge of their writing, writers were free to reconstruct the piece or make only minor changes. It was up to them. Evaluation in this sense was quite different from evaluation by a teacher.

I was surprised, week after week, at the way my words were heard by other people. Dismayed at one of the earliest meetings that my written voice sounded like "someone wearing a tweed jacket and smoking a pipe," I became cautiously inventive. I tried on a different voice. A responder told me that now I sounded more like a vice-principal in his high school. Finally I invented a lighter voice. Hearing the responders each week in the group, I began to hear their voices as I wrote. "OK, I'll give you an example," I'd say back, or I'd ask, "Can you follow this?" My responders were good company, even inside my head. Beyond that, they gave me a reason to get moving and get words down on paper. Like most writers, I needed that.

Suzanne Before the Maui Conference in 1982 I had children working together in writing groups without me. These groups were informal, usually self-selected, and typically made up of children who were friends. The children liked reading their writing to one another, liked having friends praise their work and give them ideas. I found, however, that I often had to lead a group of children who were disruptive, the ones Elizabeth Cohen (1986) would call "low status," the ones nobody ever wanted in their group. "I need to sit with you, Mrs. Brady," one said, "so I don't kick anybody." What to do with these children was a hard question. Another question was what to do when all the best writers chose to be together. And how would I have time for individual editing conferences if I had to stay in a group?

There was more to know about the dynamic of writing response groups, as I was to find out. The Maui Conference was a turning point, first because I met Suzie there and second because I was a member of a group like none I'd been part of before. This was a group led by Roger Whitlock.

After being in Roger's group for four days in a row, I saw why responders are most supportive when they respond to the writer all along the way, from the beginning point in the writing process to the ending point.

The four of us in Roger's group sat on the lanai, taking turns reading our writing in the warm, heavy air. Roger read to us the short story he was working on, which referred to a bouquet of "drooping calla lillies." Now as somebody who knew calla lillies from many years of gardening, I was struck by this phrase. Calla lillies, I was sure, never drooped. They might die, but they didn't droop. For the next day's group I ditched the piece I had been reading and brought a few paragraphs of response to Roger's bouquet. I wrote about the battle I waged as gardener-guardian. My calla lillies were defiant weeds that thrust up with abandon through rose beds and petunias. These words prompted a response from a couple of the group members that I had never expected. "Poetic," they said. "You should convert this to a poem."

To be brief, I did. Though I felt that my words were probably nothing but drivel, I thought that with the group helping me, a poem was something I could try. The group members gave me suggestions and ideas. They told me which words worked. I kept changing the poem between meetings until it finally took a shape I liked. The group acted as a powerful support, holding me up, like a would-be circus acrobat who was trying something she wouldn't otherwise have the courage to try.

I came home from Maui feeling I had to convey this supportive kind of social role to the ten-year-olds I was teaching. I wanted them to know how to encourage and help one another, as I had been encouraged and helped, and to persuade one another to take risks.

I also came home thinking about my conversations with Suzie. We had sat at the side of the pool at a point when everyone else was worn down and going home. She was asking these questions, one after another, as if it were the opening day of the conference. She didn't quit.

"How do they learn the language for commenting on one an-other's writing?" she asked. "Do you think they pick it up from you? What do they say to one another in the group when you're not there? Have you ever taped them?" When I got home, I found the questions didn't fade away as conference talk often does. Suzie's voice was right there in my ear.

<u>Suzie</u> Could children be good responders? Could they help other writers? Could being responders and practicing with others in a group lead children to assess their own writing?

Those questions were fascinating to consider partly because they ran so counter to traditional practices in the teaching of writing. In the past, writing teachers had assumed a one-to-one relationship, teacher to student: the teacher assigned the paper, collected the pa-per, wrote comments in the margins of the paper, perhaps assigned a revision, and gave a mark to the paper. Now, as *process* became a key word, and writing teachers looked increasingly to ways of helping students before they handed the paper in, we teachers thought to ourselves: "Why not bring students in on the act? Why not use more student-to-student dialogue, both to rehearse the ideas not yet on the page and to rethink those already there?"

But people were skeptical. The reason I was so bent on finding out what went on in Suzanne's writing groups was that people had real doubts about the abilities of students to give helpful response. Some saw student responders as the blind leading the blind. Others wondered how students could be expected to provide helpful re-sponse when teachers themselves wrote margin comments that left students feeling put down or mystified. How could students do better?

In my own writing classes the results of using writing groups were inconsistent. In my junior-level writing classes, almost every student embraced the spirit of Roger's ground rules, seeming to un-derstand that this give-and-take ritual gave the writer food for thought to be taken home and digested slowly. No one missed a group meeting; they were too important. Many of my freshmen, though, sounded as if they were confused by the whole idea of listening to their peers and giving response. For the first time in their lives they were paying good money to get it straight from the professor, and now I was asking them to listen to their peers.

I didn't for a minute see groups as the blind leading the blind, but theory told me that learners learn from working with someone more knowledgeable. I was convinced by the apprenticeship metaphor of teaching and learning, which argued that even when the pomp and stiffness of the lecture method were dismantled, the teacher remained central. A learner sought advice from someone who had worked in the field long enough to be skilled. The learner as apprentice did not ask for answers from another novice.

Donald Murray opted for apprenticeship in the form of one-to-one conferences, teacher to student. His article "The Listening Eye" (1979) urged writing teachers to give up their podium at the front of the room, to stop spending their nights writing margin comments, and instead to give students just fifteen minutes in a one-to-one conference to talk their way out of their difficulties. But he didn't say that the listener could be another student.

Donald Graves had much the same attitude. At the moment Suzanne and I were meeting on Maui, he was hard at work writing a book that would revolutionize the teaching of writing in elementary schools, showing teachers how to give up a correction philosophy and instead to create in their classrooms a cottage industry by having children write their own books. Graves translated the apprenticeship metaphor quite literally: work alongside the learner. In his chapter "Helping Children to Speak First" (1983) he set out ways to do this. Sit beside the child, he said, not facing the child as one would do across a table. Do all that you can to make the relationship collaborative, he advised. Avoid the temptation to take the child's paper into your own hands. Invite the child to speak first.

Neither Graves nor Murray paid great heed to collaboration among students. Graves said more on this topic than Murray, presumably because other children were a more obvious presence in an elementary classroom than they were in a professor's office. But in spite of the fact that one of his chapters was entitled "Help the Children to Help Each Other," the help he referred to was not group response to a draft. It was on-the-spot cooperation at the time of composing—for example, the help provided by Heidi when she said to her friend Cheryl (165): "Well, silly, you could put in about how we got into trouble over it. You know, your Mom!" Other teachers at the school where Graves carried out his research were more interested in children's reflective thought—in the comments they made one to another about the work in progress—than Graves was himself.

About the longer, more formal meetings of response groups, Graves was clearly negative. By way of warning, he mentioned a child who had been intimidated by the responses of his group because group members asked him too many questions. Leaving the meeting, the child could be heard muttering, "To hell with all of them; I'll do it my own way." This was a case, wrote Graves, where an audience could be intrusive and the teacher would need to limit the number of questions or at least be on hand to watch their effect on the child writer (266). Graves' commentary was an interesting reaction from someone as interested as he claimed to be in peer response. He seemed to be saying that the teacherless meeting was too "iffy" a situation: children were not mature enough to be helpful, and they might actually hurt other children.

At the time Suzanne and I talked on Maui in 1982, researchers had already begun to investigate the question of how effective children are as responders in teacherless groups. My interest was piqued by one study (Crowhurst 1979) showing that students (in this case, fifth graders) could be taught to provide supportive comments to writers in progress. When teachers worked with children (in this case, three teachers from Manitoba, Canada), the children became quite capable of (1) *encouraging*, (2) *asking for greater detail* and (3) *suggesting other improvements*. (The comments in this case were written, not oral.) Marion Crowhurst, who analyzed the children's comments, provided examples.

> Children *encouraged:* "Your story was interesting and in some places funny. I wanted to read on."

They *requested more detail:* "Why did you get a beating? How did your radio break?"

They *suggested improvement:* "Maybe you could add more at the end to tell what happens" or "One thing I noticed was that you sort of had too much dialogue and not enough telling" (759).

According to other investigations, students are good responders even when they are not insightful or perceptive about their own writing. Students working in small groups have been shown to give better response than do teachers trying to respond to twenty-five or thirty students in the class. Despite the large number of studies showing no significant differences between the responses of peers and the responses of teachers, a recent count showed seven studies in which the difference in effectiveness was clear, five favoring peer comments, and two favoring the comments of teachers. Teacher comments were more effective in matters of word choice and grammar, student comments more effective when it came to critical thinking, organization, and appropriateness. "More effective" in these studies meant that the comments were directly related to the quality of the revised text.[1]

Teachers, understandably, have not seen eye-to-eye with these results. An interesting survey conducted by Sarah Freedman of the Center for the Study of Writing (1987) showed that 560 teachers who were identified as successful teachers of writing by writing project directors clearly believed that their own responses in one-to-one conferences were better than the responses of students. I probably would have said the same myself several years ago, and I feel even now that I'm a better responder in face-to-face conferences than many of my students—not all, because some are amazingly good—but many of them.

Still, the point may be moot. The survey showed that peer response groups are more common than conferences with the teacher because teacher time is short. Said one teacher filling in Freedman's survey questionnaire: "I wish there was more time for individual writing conferences. Since there is not, I find training students to respond to each other vital!" (1987, 61).

Suzanne
··········

The year after Maui I kept thinking about Suzie's question "Have you ever taped the groups?" By this time I was really quite curious about what was going on between writer and responders. Good writing was happening, as I saw by the numbers of pieces that children wanted to publish and put in the classroom library. I had a window on the groups by way of the conversation I had with each child as we sat together one-to-one to make corrections in drafts that the groups had decided were ready for editing. In that editing role, I could ask the child, "What did your group say about this?" And if I thought the piece still had major problems, I'd say, "I don't understand such and such," and send the child back to the group for more help. So I knew, in general, how the groups were going.

I also heard children saying to one another, "We have to meet." Meeting was something I now encouraged them to do as often as every other day during the daily writing hour, even going outside the classroom door and sitting on the patio just within earshot. Having come from my meetings with Roger's group, I understood that urge to meet. But was it the same for the children as it was for me? What was being said in those meetings? I wanted to know.

Realize that the teacher part of me was standing back, looking, and seeing chaos. In the group meetings I saw laughing, acorn throwing, noise, confusion, and complaining. I saw all the disorder that, as teachers, you try not to have. So part of me said, "This better be good. This better be good, because if it isn't, I'm wasting a whole lot of time."

In the first couple of years after Maui, I did random tape recording, asking groups here and there to tape their meetings, so that I could be certain they were going well. I did not hear wonderful responses on every tape, but I heard serious effort. The children were as "on task," to use the educational community's favorite word, as my own Maui group had been. (I remember how some members of my own group had sometimes strayed from the topic, chatting about lunch or whatever.) But in both the adult and children's groups, someone would finally say, "Whose turn is it?" and that was enough to put the group back on track.

I remember, especially, the tape of Kahlil and Jeannie because Kahlil was a fourth grader in the grade four-five combination I was teaching that year, and Jeannie was a fifth grader. I was aware of the gap between fourth- and fifth-grade capabilities, yet on that tape, not only did Kahlil, the younger child, make helpful responses to Jeannie's story, but Jeannie accepted them in a perfectly serious manner. All four members of this group carried on as authors who were intent on their work.

Kahlil said that she liked the plot of Jeannie's story. She liked the names of the characters, and she wondered if the kingdom had a name. She liked the rhyming answers that the leprechaun gives Sylvia. She liked the parts where Sylvia throws all her valuables onto the ground and when she wakes up and "sees the trees are bare and everything."

She understood that Sylvia wanted revenge on the thieves, Huff and Brook, and that she lured them into the forest with the treasure map, got them drunk on wine, and then replaced the valuables in the bag with the snake. But what she didn't understand was how come— if the snake killed Huff when Huff opened the bag—the snake didn't kill Sylvia also, when Sylvia put the snake *into* the bag. In his turn, responder Mike picked up on the snake question: "You didn't tell how she holds that snake," he said. "If they (Huff and Brook) can't hold it, how can she?" Kahlil then made a suggestion: "You should say she knew how to take care of snakes because her father taught her, or a peasant taught her, something like that."

I don't remember now which of these suggestions Jeannie actually took, and I wouldn't be surprised if she left her story as it was. The value of the response should not be measured by whether it gets incorporated into the revision, though I teach the children to consider the comments in writing their next draft. A teacher from Eau Claire, Wisconsin, who also listened to tapes of her writing groups (Russell 1985), saw the effect of responding not in terms of revision but in terms of composing and having something to say. She was astonished at what happened to two of her poorest writers when they began asking questions as responders. Their own writing improved dramatically. This is what I was beginning to see myself—that as children became better responders, they became active and alive. Apparently they began to see that readers have questions and to hear those questions as they wrote.

Then something happened one day that showed me how seriously and confidently the children played their responding roles, one author to another. A reporter called to ask if she could read to the children a manuscript she was preparing to send out to publishers. As it turned out, her manuscript was a first draft and a first attempt at writing for children. Though I didn't know it at the time, it was a rather moralistic story with a little girl as the main character, an environmental theme, and talking trees. I said that a visit would be wonderful.

But I also tried to prepare the reporter. I told her how the children worked in writing response groups and that, combined into a single group, they would function as a large response group for her. She would have to read twice, and they would jot down words, and they would respond. She said that would be fine with her.

Her attitude toward the children was "aren't they cute." But for their part, the children took her seriously. When she said she wanted their help, they took that to mean that she wanted their help as responders.

So after they had listened, and jotted down words, they began to respond. First they picked out the parts they liked, which they had to search for, but they did. They liked the premise—that you should take care of the environment—so they spoke about that. Then they said things like, "This child—how old did you say this child was? It sounds as though, well, she's sitting on her mother's lap, which would make you think she's maybe four or five, yet she talks as though she is ten or eleven." Someone else said, "She sounds like a little adult." Others commented that the magical things in the story didn't make sense. One child said she knew how hard it was to do magic in a story.

The children did not say, "This is a wonderful book and I wish you well," or even "This is good. I like it." Nor did they say, "This is not very good," even though it was obvious to them that no kid was ever going to read it, not in the state it was in and that the author really needed to do another draft. So they saw themselves as helping her. She thanked them kindly, but she never came back with another draft to read. The children were puzzled by that. Their understanding—different from hers—was that you get response when you're in the middle of your project. That was the lesson I had picked up from the writing group on Maui—that you don't wait until you're finished to ask for response.

Suzie What were you doing to teach these children how to respond like this? You said earlier that you had many questions before Maui about the composition of groups and disruptive behavior, but by the time of Kahlil and Jeannie you seem more satisfied. Were you teaching differently?

Suzanne Oh yes, I had begun to teach Roger's rules of response—about reading twice, taking notes, responding in turn, and so on. That was different from what I had done earlier. I picked up a version of those same rules that had been written with an eye to fifth graders by Lynn Howgate (1983), a teacher from the Puget Sound Writing Program. Make sure the groups meet in the same place all the time, she said, and that the four members sit directly across from one another in a cross pattern. I find that these matters of ritual are effective, especially with children who are still a little scared or likely to be disruptive, because I'm saying to them, "Don't worry about the hard part, the writing and reading. Just do these easy things and you'll see how well it all turns out." There's a little magic in the ritual.

Finally, like Howgate (1983), I began to choose the groups myself, though I did not follow her advice to put all the best writers together.

Suzie Because you didn't want to group by ability?

Suzanne Because you need to spread those good writers around. The way I now group the children, there are one or two in each group who help the others. These helpers are the ones who have already been successful in writing by the time they get to fifth grade. They get what I'm talking about right away: "Oh, this is the way real writers do it—you try your writing out on readers." I remember Jane, one of these good writers from the early years when I did response groups. She said to me, with perfect clarity: "Well, if they laugh when I read it, and I want it to be funny, then I know I've done it right."

These children are ready for giving and accepting response as early as first grade. They see that writing and reading are a reciprocal thing. So if you say, "I didn't understand this part," they see how you're the reader helping the writer. They say, "Aha! Tell me what you don't understand and I'll fix that." They are the ones who see right away how responses in the group meeting can be used.

It's the other ones who need the help, the ones who don't get that central idea that you write for your readers. That simple idea isn't there for them. They just write because you're "sposta," or because the teacher says you "hafta," and they just cross their fingers and try.

Suzie   So for teaching the language of response, the most important guide is the child or children in the group who already have caught on to the writer/reader relationship. Don't you think that sounds too rosy, children being taught by children? You're the teacher. Where are you in this picture?

Suzanne   The most important guide at this point *is* the other child—and the rules, of course. Yes, I'm there, but I'm not working alongside each child. The apprenticeship metaphor does not apply here. Not only do I not have the time to work one-to-one—except when I edit pieces that will be published—but I also think that the Gravesian one-to-one style flies in the face of what I try to do, which is to create responsive children. I don't even think that the "master craftsman" role is played by the guiding children, because these children are not that skilled. These children have a kind of vision; that's what they're sharing with the others, not their skill.

Suzie   And how do they get that vision? Do they have it already when they enter the class?

Suzanne   No, not usually, but they pick it up very quickly when I say we'll be doing real writing. At the beginning of the year I say something very simple, like: "We are not going to be doing school writing in the writing hour." And then I explain what I mean by *school writing*. "School writing," I tell them, "is when I tell you what you are going to write about, and I tell you how to do it, and I tell you by a grade whether you have accomplished what I wanted you to do."

"Real writing," I tell them, "means that you decide what to write about because it's something you *want* to write about." I don't give a long speech, but that's enough for some. Like Jane, they see right away that they don't have to ask the teacher what the purpose is: they know perfectly well whether they want to make the reader laugh or scare the reader with a ghost story. So by the same token, they can figure out how to respond to somebody else. They know how to say "Yes, I saw how this was a ghost story," or "Was this a ghost story? I wasn't really sure."

Suzie   You don't give guide sheets to show children the kind of responses they should make?

Suzanne   Guide sheets contradict the whole idea that writing is for readers. When children read the guide sheet, they read the teacher's questions. When they read those questions right off the sheet, it's obvious to everyone in the group that this piece of writing is for the teacher. When I started out with teacherless groups there were lots of things I did not know about group dynamics, but I understood well that writers, no matter how young, had to feel that a piece of writing was their own and not the teacher's. I felt that handing the children my questions on a sheet of paper interfered deeply with what I was telling them about themselves as writers and readers, as people whose brains gave them power. Teaching one another was our purpose; I wanted always to demonstrate to them that this was what they were doing.

Suzie   Vision and sense of purpose, Suzanne was telling me, were prerequisite for the intuitively good group responder. Teachers couldn't go about this mechanically, teaching students what to say to one another in the group. Responders first had to know what writing was about and the purpose of what they and their classmates were writing.

As I thought about my own classes, I thought again about my freshmen, those newly arrived at the university who seemed unclear about what they were doing there and even less clear (sometimes not very curious) about the scholarly urge to ask questions and answer them. Borrowing Suzanne's idea about constructing a consciousness of shared purpose, as she had done with "smart, clever, and intelligent" and "doing real writing," I introduced to my freshmen the notion of "academic inquiry." "What does that mean?" I asked them. "What do inquirers do?" I suggested that we join the university community by becoming inquirers.

Asking questions became the means by which they did their first assignment, which was to interview a writer around campus or in the community. Questions were also the way we looked at the interview results when they came in. What did we find out in doing these interviews? What do writers in this community actually write? What, by inference, should freshmen learn to write?

Seeing that academics write to one another about the public world, about culture, current trends, and so forth, I had the students make short presentations to the class about items in the newspaper that they had selected, and pose their own thought questions about these stories. Class members were invited to help the presenter by asking their own questions, a process that enabled the presenter to select a topic for a writing project that had aroused interest. Then I did what Suzanne did in her investigative projects: I had each group member ask the other group members for additional questions on his or her own newspaper story, which they could incorporate into their project or ignore as they chose.

Midway into the semester I introduced four questions that I claimed were basic to academic inquiry: What is your argument? What are your reasons for your argument? What is your supporting evidence for your reasons? And what are the basic assumptions or values behind your argument? Since this was the time of the Persian Gulf war, I took a topical question—should the media be censored in time of war?—and worked out on the blackboard the answers that might be given to the four questions by people who had different points of view on the role of media in covering government. We did this a couple of times with different topics. Each time, the students wrote up the analysis after we worked it out on the board. Finally they returned to topics of their choice, this time posing their own controversial question and working out the analysis from materials they found.

The students asked their own questions, but they had to ask the teacher's four basic questions as well. They had to write me notes in the margin of their paper that said, "Here is my argument, here are my reasons," and so forth, drawing arrows so I couldn't miss any-thing. They drew the arrows and wrote the margin notes in class on the day the papers were due. At the same time, they wrote me a "rap sheet," talking to me about their process of writing the paper, in-cluding their intentions and the way those intentions had worked out. (The textbook for the course was *A Community of Writers* (Elbow and Belanoff 1989).)

I found that within this course frame, the small-group meetings became important to the students. My demonstrations of group meeting procedures were the same as always, and I got about the same quality of writing, or rather the same range in quality, as I or-dinarily received. But the student ratings of the course, and partic-ularly of the small-group work, were right off the charts. The difference was in the students' awareness of what they were about; they felt in control. Looking back, I realized that this semester, un-like earlier ones, I had taken time in the course to construct a sense of purpose with the students, and by using the key words of the course again and again, had woven the group work into that purpose.

Suzanne How ironic. Suzie was putting to work the idea of group members at
the college level helping each other with question asking when, in
fact, I had gotten the idea in the first place from John Wilkes, a university faculty member at Santa Cruz. Ideas traveled up and down
age levels with great ease once those of us who taught these levels
were pulled together. I thought about how Suzie and I had been
pulled together because we both had been members of a writing
group with Roger Whitlock, and about how fifth-grade teacher Lynn
Howgate, whose rules for Elbow groups for fifth graders I had borrowed, had worked on groups with a professor at the University of
Washington, Ann Ruggles Gere, the funny thing being that Ann Ruggles Gere (1987) first joined an Elbow group herself with—guess
who—Roger Whitlock. That was when Roger spent a year in Washington. I thought of how Donald Murray used to have brown-bag
lunches with Donald Graves and others in the New Hampshire
group. All of us were stimulated by working together, talking, being
face-to-face. In this atmosphere, knowledge was not just shared; it
was made.

   This atmosphere is what I remember most about my first writing
project. Everybody sat around the table talking, having differences of
opinion, some saying "I don't know about that." Project Director Don
Rothman every once in a while said something wonderful, but he
didn't lead the way and say, "This is what we're doing." He'd say,
"What are we going to do and how are you going to help us do that?"
He assumed that we were serious in our purpose and that we intended to contribute. Everyone had to give presentations, and there
was anxiety, but that anxiety felt good. Don also had a library full of
books. He assumed that, as project participants, you'd be so interested that you'd take them home and read them all night long, which,
of course, everyone did. Why? Because then you could come back
and talk about them; because you were sharing your knowledge.

   Then we'd read our writing, which was something we were hesitant about. "I know this isn't very good," someone might say just

before reading. Or someone might ask, "Do I have to be the one to read after Don?" (This is the "prefacing" that Roger talks about.) But we became more confident about our writing, and frequently people read things that would just knock your socks off.

We also tackled issues faced by the teachers in our group—bilingual education, racism, apathy, and change. "This," I thought to myself, "is the kind of class I'd like to teach." I was learning from the books, of course, but I was learning more, I think, from watching the way the group worked together. That was several years before Maui, and that experience was why I was so willing to learn more about groups later on and why I would put up with noise, confusion, and even acorn throwing.

Suzie   Nine years after Maui, in November 1991, I sat in a hotel room in Seattle with Suzanne, Marilyn, and Ellen, all the fifth-grade teachers of Monte Vista School. Marilyn had worked with Suzanne for nearly ten years, overhauling her own writing program at the same time Suzanne overhauled hers. Ellen approached the two of them only a few years ago: "I want to do what you're doing. Could I snoop around your rooms?" Now the four of us were taking a break from meetings of the huge National Council of Teachers of English (NCTE) convention.

"Remember how we used to teach paragraphs?" Marilyn asked, shaking her head. She was holding the Preface of our manuscript in her hand, reading aloud the sentence: *Teachers sometimes save children from complexity to ensure neatness and good spelling.* "That's exactly what we were doing," she said.

"They'd say to you, 'How many sentences does it have to be?'" said Suzanne, laughing.

"Oh they knew it had to be five," said Marilyn.

"They knew the rules. You could write a paragraph about how you love your mother or write a paragraph about, you know, your trip to the beach. You make it four or five sentences, indent it, punctuate it at the end, and you get a smiling face, or a 'good,' or whatever."

"It's hard," said Ellen, "to know how to get out of that whole teaching mode."

"Changing *is* chaos," said Marilyn, shaking her head again. "See, Suzie, you have to remember, I was a teacher in the old parochial school. I had prided myself on my wonderful discipline and everybody else prided me on it. And I did love to teach writing, and I thought I did a good job. Then Suzanne was coming around with this excitement in her voice, and I love learning something new, so she convinced me to go to the writing project, and then she came in and helped me organize. But to have all this noise and chaos was very trying, especially when I didn't know what was happening in the groups."

"The noise didn't bother me," said Ellen. "But I don't like feeling disorganized in my own planning. Without the two of you telling me how to go step-by-step, I really would not have been able to do this."

"But you do this differently from me," Suzanne protested.

"Yes, but I had your model to follow. That made things a whole lot easier."

My old question from Maui came back to me: "How do you teach them what to say in the writing group?" I was well aware now that such teaching could never be a mechanical process, and that teacher guide sheets prescribing set questions would not do. Constructing consciousness and setting up shared purpose came first. But what of the step-by-step that Ellen was talking about? I thought again of the first day of school. A teacher had to start somewhere. My question "How do you teach them?" had been answered in general terms. Now I wanted the rest of the picture.

NOTE

1. For studies showing the effectiveness of peer response, see Ford (1973), Sager (1973), Benson (1979), Karengianes, Pascarella, and Pflaum (1980), and Nystrand (1986). For studies showing the effectiveness of teacher response, see Boss (1987), and Yaronczyk (1990). I am indebted to Su-yueh Huang's complete review of the literature on peer response groups in her forthcoming dissertation. (S. Jacobs)

FIVE

Teaching the Language of Response

Suzie   To teach children what to say in a writing response group, Suzanne does nothing less than teach children a vision of writing and a vision of response. Teaching to "the social side of the brain," she goes beyond teaching procedural rules. She cooks up interest on the part of those children who begin the year with neither enthusiasm for writing nor an understanding of writing for readers. Ellen was thinking of these children when she asked, "How do you start?" In this chapter Suzanne answers that question. She describes her *scaffold* for the writing response group.

     The word *scaffold*, first used by Wood, Bruner, and Ross (1976), is loosely defined as "support for the learner." The term kept the two of us talking for some time and turned out to be important in our thinking, especially our thinking about how to answer a teacher's question for the "step-by-step." Ellen didn't want a recipe; she wanted a scaffolding technique. The term has caused enough confusion in the literature on teaching that we wish, in order to explain its usefulness and avoid adding confusion, to say how the two of us came to define it.

I was introduced to the word by the members of my study group at the University of Hawaii, especially by Alison Adams, a faculty member from the Department of Psychology. The six of us who met in this group, all faculty who came from departments of psychology, English, education, English as a second language, and anthropology, came to call ourselves HART, the Hawaii Association for Research in Thinking. To the other five of us in the group, Alison represented psychology and learning theory.

Meeting on Friday afternoons, munching cookies and drinking coffee in a conference room, we came to see scaffolding in terms informed by Vygotskian learning theory and by the investigations that each of us had carried out, including Alison's. (See works authored by Adams (1986), by Bayer (1990), by Brandt (1990), by Jacobs (1990), by Levin (1987), by Scribner (1990), and by Watson-Gegeo (1986).) Vygotsky was a figure who was attractive to all of us because he was the first of the major learning theorists to say something sensible about the place of the teacher. Skinner and Piaget, those learning theorists most prominent in our reading, had said nothing that helped us understand the problems of teacher role. Skinner made the teacher into a reinforcer of conditioned responses. Piaget, for all his insight into cognition, painted no teacher into the scene whatsoever.

Guided by Vygotsky's interest in the *assisted learner,* Alison had studied the ways in which parents assisted their toddlers when they took them on their laps and played the game of looking at picture books (Adams and Bullock 1986). What she found was that the middle-class parents in her study followed an amazingly patterned way of behaving. To teach the children how to play their part in the ritual of turning the pages and naming the animals pictured in the book, the parents created a scaffold. They made sure that looking at the picture was a joint activity. They made it easy for the child to join in, even at the beginning when they might have to play the child's part almost entirely. Then gradually they "upped the ante," expecting a bit more from the child with each occasion, until the child had internalized the language of the conversation and the game itself. At that point the child could identify the pictures and play the game with competence, so the support offered by the adult—in the form of partial answers, leading questions, or hints—could be withdrawn. The scaffold could come down.

Karen talked to us about scaffolding in the Solomon Islands, where she observed older siblings and parents making it possible for the very young ones to help out with gardening (Watson-Gegeo 1990). Paula's interviews of Hawaiian parents revealed ways in which they scaffolded the routines of cooking and doing chores around the house (Levin 1990). In each case, learning resulted from the child's internalization of a "game," a ritual, or a routine. In each case the older person, perhaps without realizing it, built an enabling scaffold to support the learner's initial efforts.

Scaffolding by a teacher in a classroom was a puzzle for us, however. We had trouble deciding what it looked like, primarily because we could not see a very clear similarity between what the parent could do one-to-one and what the teacher could do, one to twenty-five or thirty. We did not like the models outlined in the literature on scaffolding in the classroom. One of these, for example, was the card method, which was used in the teaching of writing (Scardamalia, Bereiter, and Steinbach 1984). Each child was given a pack of cards, and on each card was a question, such as "Can you give an example? What is the cause?" The young writer feeling the need for assistance was supposed to pick up and consult these cards in the process of writing. However, this seemed to us a scripted approach and unlikely to help. Other scaffolds (for instance, Palinscar and Brown 1984) also depended on scripting by the teacher. The guide sheet for the writing response group was yet another case of scripting.

Ann, who taught in the University of Hawaii's College of Education, and Betsy, who worked as a psychologist for the Hawaii

Department of Education, both argued that the scripting approach worked against the spirit of collaboration (Bayer 1990, and Brandt 1990). The very purpose of scaffolding was to invite collaboration—or joint participation. Why defeat that purpose?

On the phone I described our HART conversations to Suzanne. She agreed with Betsy and Ann. "Above all, I want to cultivate a sense of ownership," she said. "The small group discussions *belong* to the children. That's why I have to stay out. That's why I don't suggest questions for them to ask. They need to feel they control those conversations."

"But you suggest the kinds of good questions they might ask."

"That's when we're talking about the idea of good questions. That's when we're having a whole-class discussion about that concept, which is very different from saying to them, 'Now I suggest that you ask this question in your small-group meeting.'"

The others in the HART meeting were interested in Suzanne's reactions. Dennis Searle had reacted similarly to an instance of teacher scaffolding (1984). In that case, a teacher "helped" a small child in the midst of a sharing routine by stopping her to ask questions. In the name of "helping," the teacher had taken the floor, said Searle, thereby interfering with the sense of ownership that children normally feel when they play a role during the morning "sharing."[1]

Suzanne   For all the trouble over its definition, I was intrigued by the idea of the scaffold. It helped me think about a problem I had noticed in a workshop that I gave for other teachers. To one of these workshops I took a videotape of my children working in writing response groups. I had made the tape in a hurry only the week before, which was sometime in December. To make the tape, I had set up the camcorder on a tripod and let it run while I was doing something else.

The teachers and I viewed the tape and talked about the groups. They found these interesting. But then several of them said, "Your children are different. Mine would not be able to sit there and listen and make all these responses without me sitting in."

My children were not different, I was sure of that. But I realized I had made a mistake by making it appear to the teachers that I was nowhere in the picture, as though all I had to do was to tell the children what to do in the group and they did it. This particular tape was misleading, given the fact that in September and October I had been right at center stage, and that even after that I had helped the children with the writing groups, though not by sitting in. The concept of scaffolding would help me explain both my presence and my disappearance. It would help me show how and when I withdrew my visible self.

Now when I talk to teachers, I always use the scaffolding metaphor to represent teacher support. Scaffolds, I say, are temporary structures used by construction workers while building. Workers put the scaffolds up, and then they take them down. The scaffold provides support while something new is under construction. Then, lo and behold, when the workers remove the scaffold, the work stands by itself. The observer who comes along later may never know that a scaffold once was there; observers see only the finished work—in this case, never seeing the scaffolder at work on the writing group verbal routine.

Suzie   It was Ann who really got me thinking about the importance of key concepts. An important element in the scaffold that she had developed for university students was the *anchor*. Anchors were words that she and the students attached to meanings that they constructed jointly as they talked together and read their writing in small groups. Anchors kept the memory of that process of joint construction alive, kept it from floating away with the passage of time. Ann said she kept these anchoring words at the forefront of everybody's attention. She kept bringing them up. As time passed, the words became increasingly meaningful to the students.

Talking with Suzanne, I heard a similar theme. "What I do," she said, "is raise consciousness."

"And how do you do that?" I asked.

"With words," she said.

That's when we started to talk about *smart, clever,* and *intelligent,* the words that she kept bringing up. Each time the children returned to the words, they folded the experience of their ongoing work back into the meaning of those words. The words, in turn, created a conscious sense of self. "Who am I? I'm Intelligent."

I returned to the puzzle of how to define scaffolding. As a concept, it was worth the trouble. I valued it for a number of reasons that I became aware of as I conversed both with Suzanne and my HART group. This concept put the teacher in the educational picture. It put collaboration in a good light. It also put risk taking in a good light, since we could now talk about support and making it easy in those situations that, like writing, we recognized as risky. And it focussed attention on the teacher's changing presence.

The classic definition of scaffolding, the one described earlier in connection with Alison's study of parents and toddlers, had a number of key points worth noting. Scaffolding was a way of inviting participation in a routine, by offering structured support, then gradually upping the ante, until the routine itself could be internalized, and the scaffold taken down. To these points I now added three more:

1. Key words were crucial.
2. The teacher needed to come to the front of the room to lead children in making connections between the words and their ongoing experience.
3. Ownership by learners was essential, which explained why it was important for children to control the discourse of their small groups.

Suzanne   I now spend the first six weeks of school building a scaffold for the language of response. I show the children from the first day of school that writing and response go together like two people having a conversation. I have them begin with journals—writing, reading aloud, and talking back to the writer. I keep on with the journal every day for six weeks, and at the same time I move the children into two other writing tasks—interviewing and word pictures—which show them how to work with others in slightly different ways. Writing is social from beginning to end.

Here is what I do on the first day.

I hand each child a composition book, saying "This is your journal for the year. In your journal you'll make a history of your life as a fifth grader."

Then I ask them all to write. They can write about how they feel, I tell them, about coming to school on the first day and finding that their best friend has moved away, or about how they missed breakfast and now they're hungry. I provide enough suggestions to make them understand that the choice of topic is really theirs. I tell the second-language children that they can write in their first language if they want to, then I myself begin to write. I scribble, stare out the window, chew on my pencil, and generally behave like a writer for about seven minutes.

Not every child follows suit. Some whisper and some just watch, until I say, "Two minutes left!" Then every hand writes something on the page. Maybe it's the first-day honeymoon. The children will do almost anything a teacher asks of them on that day, even if they're scared and don't think they can write.

Next comes reading aloud, one-by-one. I give my little talk about how I used to be afraid to jump off the diving board; how I'd always back off the board and climb down the ladder until one day a bunch of kids lined up behind me and I couldn't back off. I jumped, I tell them, and it was easier after that. I wasn't so scared.

We sit in a circle on the rug, ready or not, and everybody reads. A volunteer begins, someone whose courage is recognized, and then we go on around the circle. If someone has written in a foreign language, we listen with great interest and ask to see the writing. I also read out my own first-day apprehensions and aspirations.

Next comes responding, which I initiate and which some of the children add to as we go around the circle, though I don't require this from everyone. After each child reads, I say what the writer's words remind me of, or make me think. "I went to the Santa Cruz Beach and Boardwalk too," I'll say, "but I was afraid to go on the roller coaster." Class members murmur their own comments.

"The line was too long. My mom wouldn't wait."

"It's too scary for me."

By acknowledging the life of the writer, we become a community of writers. That's an important part of response: acknowledgment.

Suzie   How long does it take to go around the circle? Do you do this every day? Once a week? Don't the children get fidgety, listening to all the others?

Suzanne   No, they honestly do not fidget. They listen to every child, all the way around the circle, which on the first day might take about forty-five minutes. Whatever the reason—maybe it's the first-day honeymoon again—they listen. Then, after the first few days, they're hooked. They *want* to hear.

We carry out the same routine day after day, for the first six weeks. We call it the "writing time" hour. After the beginning of November, we keep the same daily hour for writing but spend only one day a week in the journal routine. We spend two of the other four days on individual writing and two on writing response groups.

During these first six weeks, the journal routine creates a life of the class—an ongoing history. Personal stories have a way of getting started, then getting updated in the journal day after day, like soap operas. Class news is generated and broadcast. The resulting intimacy lays the groundwork for the response groups. In no way could I cut off the routine after the first six weeks; this is why we continue once a week, from November through the rest of the year. A side benefit of the journal is that I can read out my own feelings, and I may even use it to complain about something going on in the class, in a way I don't like doing from the front of the room.

For example, I may read out my comments on name calling. I may say that I remember when people used to call me names, especially when I was still short, and my feet were already the size they were going to be when I grew up. They were long, really long. I knew that. Nobody had to remind me. And I remember how it hurt when kids made fun of them.

Suzie   Do the children ever complain about anything? Do they say they don't want to share something because it's too private?

Suzanne   Surprisingly, they don't, but I make a point of privacy. Early in the year, after I see that everyone is comfortable reading, I will say, when it is my turn to read, "This journal entry is not appropriate for me to read aloud." They look at me with great curiosity, but they understand. After that, every now and then, one of the children will use that permission not to read. Sometimes, if a child is reading about private family matters, I will say, "I don't think that's appropriate for us to hear."

But other than these times, the journal writing is public writing, in keeping with the classroom idea that hiding the self is hardly ever—and sharing is almost always—a good idea.

Suzie   What about revision? How do you teach them to go beyond correcting and rethink what they have written? I don't suppose they revise their journals.

Suzanne   No, I don't have them revise journals, which are strictly for their history as a class.

I build up to the whole idea of revision gradually. I up the ante, expecting more of them as we go along. Here is where the key words *respond* and *revise* come in, and also where I go beyond my initial role as joint participant. Now I begin a different phase of scaffolding—one devoted more to consciousness raising. I come to the front of the room at this point, after they have finished a joint activity, and I ask them to look back at what they've just finished doing, and to think again about the meaning of *respond* and *revise*. I ask them to reflect.

I begin with a simple idea: "Revision is something two people who are both involved in a piece of writing do together." Then I take them through two activities, the "Interview" and "Word Pictures."

For the interview project, each child interviews and writes up a profile of another child. Each child also draws a portrait of the partner. Then, before writing the final draft, the child consults with the interviewee on details that should be changed or added. The interviewee, as the subject of the writing, is sure to suggest changes. This is a case where the writer and the responder both have a stake in getting the words right, so when I ask them to be responders, they find it easy and natural to take on the role.

Once finished, the profiles are used by the writers to introduce their responder-partners to the class.

> Jenny Roth moved to Monterey from Texas this summer. It was a long trip. She had to sit in the back seat with her brother, who is a brat, and her cat named Tiger. They moved here because . . .
>
> Mrs. Brady is a grandmother. Her grandchildren are Jacob and Kiara, age nine, Ryan age seven, Leslie age six and Kristine age five. The oldest one is Gary age thirteen, now in seventh grade. She was born many years ago in Rhode Island.

The portraits are displayed, with great hilarity, as each team of writers takes the authors' chairs to read the profiles. Then the profiles and portraits are published as a class book, which the children periodically leaf through and talk about. When a new person joins the class, a new profile is written, drawn, and placed in the book. The first in a series of classroom productions, the book becomes a marker of class identity and tangible proof of collaboration in writing.

It's important to understand how the interview is part of the overall scaffolding of response. For one thing, it extends the idea of joint participation—writing as a game that brings people into contact with one another—which is the idea of the journal routine as well. Both the journal and the interview make it clear that writing pulls us together as a class and makes us notice one another. The interview makes each child the object of attention, first of one other person and then of the whole class. The class itself becomes the object of attention as the class book is displayed prominently and repeatedly referred to.

The interview project works as a scaffolding of response in another way: it makes the meanings of *respond* and *revise* completely clear. When the partners work together, responders have no problem deciding what to say. "You want the profile to say everything important about you," I tell the children. "So what should you do as a responder? Help your partner by adding things. What should you do once your partner makes suggestions? Add those things in. That's revising." Probably the hardest part of accepting response is realizing that it's help, not correction. The whole project makes help easy to give and easy to take.

The second project, the writing of "word pictures," is a way to up the ante (see Figure 5–1). At this point I make the task more difficult and the process of revision more complex. *Word picture* is my term for an imagistic poem, such as Sandburg's "Fog." Although I don't use the word *poem,* since for fifth graders poems must rhyme, I've found that word pictures are full of potential for inventive minds. I use a word picture exercise to show the children how they can play with words they've already written—cutting, adding, and placing them differently on the page, almost as they would the objects in an art project. The key word *revision* can now be seen in a new light. When it comes time to revise, I sit with each child in a very brief conference, during which I take a rather active hand in suggesting how the child might move words around, place them differently on the page, or make additions.

There are three parts to this project: (l) brainstorming and writing the first draft, (2) meeting with me to revise, and (3) making final revisions and a final draft.

To begin this project, I keep alert for some shared visual experience, such as the uprooting of the lawn outside our window by workmen installing a new drain system, or the emergence of the monarch butterflies from cocoons in the classroom, or the heavy fog that everyone in Monterey knows well. I talk about using words to recreate pictures and the feelings that go with them. We brainstorm these words on the chalkboard, and then I compose two or three word pictures on the board in front of the children. The important part is to show them how my mind is working as I do this.

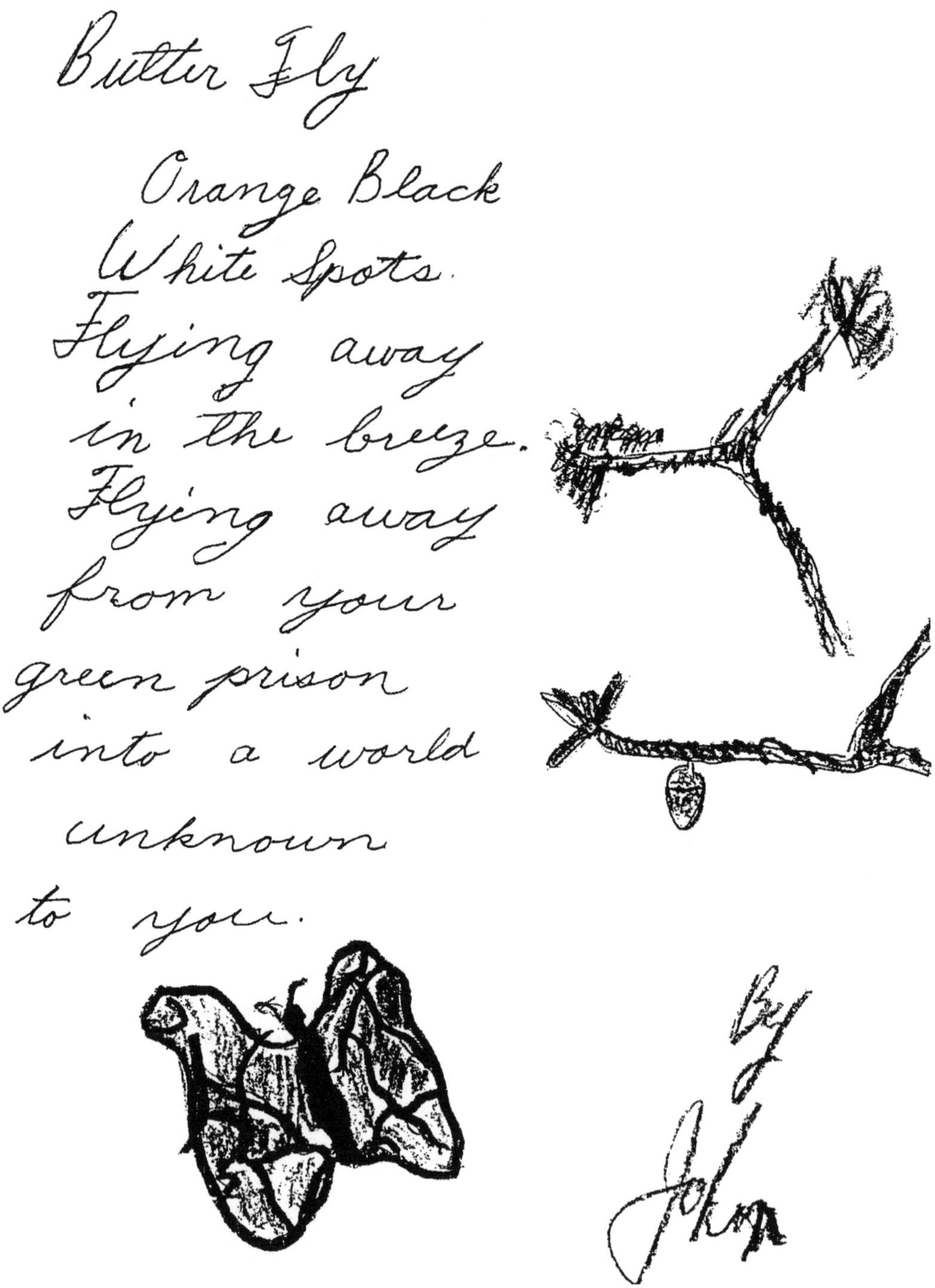

Butter Fly

Orange Black
White Spots.
Flying away
in the breeze.
Flying away
from your
green prison
into a world
unknown
to you.

By
John

FIGURE 5–1   John's Word Picture

Take the experience of fog, for example. I'll stand at the board writing as I think to myself out loud:

> I always say "oh no" when I see it in the morning because I don't like having the world disappear. I think I'll use "gone" or maybe "disappeared." How about "where is the world?" Do I need a question mark here? "Gone." I'll have that word by itself. Let's see, I'll show a picture: "woolly and gray." Good word, "woolly." Maybe a question mark after "gone." Would I like another "gone" after that? or maybe "disappeared." What do you think? What else could I say?

And so we talk through the composing using different feeling words, and I ask, "Did I capture that emotion? Can you feel what I felt? Can you see what I saw? Are the words making that picture?"

I've placed the words in different patterns so that the children can see that the arrangement doesn't look like a prose form. Then I show them some pages of poetry—being very careful not to say we are writing poetry—just to show other ways of placing words. Then we reread the pieces on the board and decide we are reasonably satisfied with them. I say they are going to write some word pictures of their own. And then I erase the board.

Tension. How do they know "what I want" if there isn't something to copy? Children who in the past have used "word banks"—teacher-constructed word lists—now have no bank of words to consult. Were they supposed to remember them? What about spelling? My task now is to soothe. "You don't want to write mine. You want to write yours. We'll worry about spelling later. When I brainstormed, I thought about what was important to me. What was *your* experience with fog? Try out different things. Write a bunch of them. Some you'll like and some you won't. Read them to your neighbor."

This project ups the ante, marking a break from the writing of the journal and the interview, both of which were free in form and therefore easy to write. The revising in the interview project was merely a matter of making the changes requested by the partner.

The children all write about the same thing, and they share their work as they go along, but the task requires them to look inward as well, and to make choices that might be different from those of other people.

I flit around the room offering encouragement but never lighting long enough for a real conference. "Ahhh," I say. "Looks good." "Read that to Rachel." "Two already!" And "All the fog's outside, no fog in these brains." The writers persistently ask one question: "Is this OK?"

"Looks good to me," I answer. I slow down and become quiet. Writing really takes over. This is fun. I hear them reading to each other. A few announce that they're finished. "Put your name on them," I say "and put them in your desks. I'll meet with each one of you during the week and we'll see how to revise them."

In the case of word pictures, I show that response is useful at two points: during brainstorming, when the children show their first efforts to their team members, and later, between drafts, when the first draft is finished and the final draft not completed. It's important to say that in the end the writing belongs to the writer; so even when I make suggestions, I make sure they have a time to consider these suggestions and decide for themselves which changes they want to make.

Collecting all their finished word pictures into a class book is essential; why do revisions if no audience will appreciate them? I make sure to place a few blank pages in the back, then place this book, along with the interview book, on the shelf at the back of the room. There the children periodically leaf through the books, write responses to other children's work, and look to see whether other children might have written responses to theirs.

By this time the class has a shared meaning for the concepts "revise" and "respond." We've used these labels repeatedly as we've gone through these joint activities: the journals, the interviews, and the word pictures. I've labeled nothing "right" or "wrong." There were no grades, and no one died when they didn't do it "my way." They've learned to look for authority elsewhere—to themselves as revisers and to other children as responders.

Suzie   I notice that you've had all the children write on the same topic in the "fog" exercise, which is something that Graves would probably disapprove of. You don't think the children should always choose their own topics?

Suzanne   Once we've passed the first six weeks, after their Halloween stories, the children choose their own topics. But early in the year, because it's so crucial for them to walk through the stages of response and revision and find out what these words mean, I don't want to have everybody working on something different. Some children need the permission to do pretty much the same as someone else is doing or what I demonstrated on the board. At this point, their ability to choose their own topic is not my priority. Social role is my priority.

Suzie   So at this point, since they know their social role as responders, they're ready for the teacherless group?

Suzanne   No, not really. I do a couple more things intended to raise their consciousness of the responder's role. We keep going back to the word *responder* and talking about what it means. We have discussions about this.

Sometimes I set up an elaborate activity just to prepare for a discussion. I've done this, for example, with the help of a kindergarten teacher whose room was empty of children in the afternoon but full of blocks. I owe this idea to Lisa Meckel, herself a kindergarten teacher for many years. I sent my children to her room, one group at a time, telling them that they should build something and give it a name. Though a little uncertain why fifth graders should be playing with blocks, the children nevertheless built with gusto, putting up, taking down, admiring, viewing from various perspectives, and talking to one another all the while. The kindergarten teacher surreptitiously took notes on the language used by the children while working, then took an instant photo of them and their named creation before they returned. As each group came back, I tacked up the photos on the bulletin board and wrote the name of the creation underneath.

In the discussion that followed, we said how block building and writing were similar. An obvious point, since they had just titled their block creation, was that both written and block-built creations were given titles by inventive people. People always seemed to be naming things, and they always seemed able to come up with words for this purpose—that is, if they were thinkers.

Another point, in both writing and block building, is that the talk of the group makes the task easier and more fun.

Another is that the vision of another person is helpful. When something is under construction, you need another person's eyes. The other person may notice what's there and can name it, whether it's a roof, a catwalk, or a bit of foreshadowing.

Another is change. For both block builders and writers, change is a normal part of the construction process. Change is creative rather than destructive. Change is for improving, not just correcting. When I read out the words used by the children and copied by the kindergarten teacher, we realize that many of them could have been used by writers in progress: "Let's change this part . . . Let's look at it from this side . . . Let's move this around." Most of the children catch on to the idea that whole walls of their stories can also be torn down and rebuilt. The blocks metaphor is fruitful, living in the children's memories all year long.

Suzie   I don't think we give children enough credit for their ability to think in abstractions. In that discussion, they're using language in abstract ways.

Suzanne   And I expect them to apply abstractions. For example, I direct them to "praise" and "encourage" in their role as responder. These are words that I teach. Remember that these are kids from everywhere, many of them wrenched from family networks that they might have been part of somewhere else. We're talking about relationships and the quality of these relationships, but particularly the quality of their working relationships. Many of the children have little experience with sibling cooperation.

I have a whole routine now for teaching "praise" and "encourage." The last of the activities I use for teaching the language of response, this routine begins when all the children in the school are engrossed in the goriness of Halloween. Halloween is in the stores, the media, the stories we're reading in school, everywhere. Spiders are spinning, blood is dripping, trapdoors are opening, and heads are rolling. In the middle of all this, I have them draw a picture. I ask them to imagine a haunted house, then to imagine themselves walking up the steps to the front door, then to imagine that they open the door and look in. They should draw what they see. Then, when they have finished the drawing, I have them write a story, reading bits of it to their teammates as they go along (see Figure 5–2).

We stop before anyone says, "I'm finished," and at this point I begin a discussion about the quality of the helping relationship.

I read to them a few Halloween stories written by third graders and shared with me by their teacher. I present them as fine examples of third-grade work, an evaluation that the fifth graders are glad to agree with. Then I ask them to praise the work. "I'll carry your comments back to the third graders," I tell them. "Be specific, and let them know what you are praising. Let them know what they've done well."

"That's easy," someone says. "The werewolf was funny when he got stuck in the door." "*Horrible* was a great word to use," says someone else. This is praise. Pointed praise and praise that "points" to particular words. The children are pleased with themselves for passing their wisdom on to the little kids.

"Now," I say, "suppose we wanted to turn these third-grade stories into fifth-grade stories. How could we do that? Suppose these writers put their stories in a drawer and brought them out again when they were in the fifth grade. What advice could we give them then? What encouragement could they use to rewrite these stories as fifth graders?"

It was Friday, Halloween night. It was pitch black except for moonlight. I stared at the full moon shining through the mist and clouds.

I was in the car with my babysitter on the way to go trick-or-treating with some kids she knew.

I was dressed as the Grim Reaper. I had a black cloak on. I also had a plastic sickle. Of course my parents wouldn't let me have a real one.

(from *The House* by Ted Maruyama)

Her parents and brother were with an old man. They were all watching T.V. They all had this blue see-through-ish look. The old man looked at her and red lasers came out of his eyes, a green mist swirled around her and Kelly became very small and walked on all fours.

(from *The Dream Was (Or Wasn't It?)* by Katelin B. Collord)

Then all of a sudden he yelled, "I'm out of gas!" We started to lose altitude and fell into a pumpkin patch. Colin fell on a pumpkin in a way that he couldn't get it off his head. Finally the pumpkin fell off all by itself. While that was happening Super Mike was refilling his jet engine with his spare tank of fuel. All of a sudden we heard this wicked kind of laughing coming from behind us. We turned around and saw the ghoul.

(from *The Ghoul With the Checkered Pants* by Sean Rigmaiden)

FIGURE 5–2   Excerpts from Published Halloween Stories

That's also easy. "One story didn't really end. It just stopped and said *The End*." We talk about that. It's no longer appropriate to use *The End* instead of really ending, but endings are hard to do. Should we tell the author how to end the story? Someone says that sounds bossy, which is something to think about. One story had an elaborate illustration necessary for understanding the action. Could the author also use words?

Could encouraging the authors to consider these possibilities make terrific fifth-grade work out of terrific third-grade work? "Praise" and "encouragement" are ways to think about response. The human element—the "who" behind the response, why someone would want this response, and how that person might use this response—is something I now realize I can teach.

Suzie   I notice you're quite firm in saying "before anyone says *I'm finished."* Are you thinking of your own experience—the fact that you needed response before you were finished?

Suzanne   I've found that waiting until the first draft is finished before having others respond smacks of correction. It says, "This is what is wrong with your work." *Finished* means just what it says: "reluctant to hear genuine feedback," in the manner of the would-be children's author who visited the class. That was my own reaction to feedback before I met Roger and participated in his groups. I wasn't sure I wanted it. I discovered I needed the group most while I was still wrestling with a piece. The group's thinking helped my thinking. A finished draft made me think of response as "judgment." An unfinished draft made me see response as "encouragement."

Suzie   So you've been shaping the children's thinking about their social role in a working relationship by teaching them the words *respond* and *revise, praise* and *encourage*.

Suzanne   Do I "teach" these words? I don't think so. I make sure that we discuss them. But the children work out meanings for themselves. They start using the words because I've introduced them, but the meaning is something that comes to them over time. That's why, after we start the groups, we have to keep coming back to "what is response?" so they can discuss their ongoing experiences in the group. They're still figuring out what "response" is.

Suzie   You're ready, now, to start the group meetings?

Suzanne   Yes.

Suzie   And what do you tell them about how to proceed?

Suzanne   I go over the rules of procedure:

> Decide on a meeting place (somewhere away from the desks)
> Put chairs in a cross pattern and sit with knees almost touching
> Always sit in the same order
> Bring writing folder for lap desk, extra paper and pencil for responses
> Chairperson begins the meeting and reads first.

We practice them with one writing group as a model, then I say, "Go to it. Take turns reading your Halloween story aloud. Your responders will respond." Then I add, "Cooperation is key."

Suzie   That's all?

Suzanne   That's enough to get them started. Whatever they still need to learn about the social role of the responder is not something they can learn in a moment or two before sitting down in the group. But they've been rehearsing and discussing the social role for several weeks. Now is the time to try out what they've learned.

NOTE

1. See also Freedman (1987, 8), who makes a point of not using the term *scaffold,* Newkirk (1989, 142–43), who has reservations about the term, and Stone (1989), who feels there is something missing in the metaphor. The HART group had similar reservations about the version of *reciprocal teaching* described in Palinscar and Brown (1984). (S. Jacobs)

SIX

Writing Groups in Action

Suzanne In spite of my scaffolding efforts, I couldn't be sure that the writing response groups were effective. Suzie had asked me at the Maui conference, "What do they say to each other in the groups?" I didn't really know. Once I put the groups to work on their own, my only way of assessing their worth was to interview children when they came to me for their one-on-one help with editing, after they had already read their writing in the group meeting. "What did the group have to say?" I would ask. The children's answers were not very articulate, so at that point I remembered Suzie's question: had I ever taped the group meetings? In this way, I began to evaluate my attempts to make writing a social affair.

In 1983, I began randomly taping a few meetings with my two tape recorders, with fascinating results. Marilyn and I spent hours talking about these, and I went into her classroom, too, to tape some of her groups. Still, my questions were not answered. I needed to hear not just a few meetings but a sequence of meetings so that I could judge how the children changed. I needed to hear all the groups, not just some of them.

At that time, California began granting money to school districts for teacher-mentor programs. I applied to this program and began to work as a mentor with teachers interested in writing, several of whom were interested in the idea of writing groups. They were curious to hear what went on in my classroom. With the mentoring budget, I bought enough additional recorders and tapes so that the next year, every response group could tape itself for every meeting. From November to April, seven groups met twice a week for about forty-five minutes. I listened to the tapes after school, in the car, and at home in the evening, wearing a little button in my ear while doing the dishes. My husband, the cook, began to doubt whether I heard anything he ever said. At any rate, I heard what the children said to each other when I wasn't in the group. I heard their stories, questions, giggles, and occasional squabbles. Though they were aware that I was listening, they seemed remarkably unaffected. I strained to hear their voices, which had been recorded over the whine of electric saws and the banging of hammers at a nearby construction project. Most of the classroom groups met just outside the classroom door in a small patio area. The children seemed not to be bothered by the noise.

Listening to all of this, I had to laugh. The opening meetings were rather stiff affairs. Each responder, in turn, would ask the writer a single question, and then the chair of the group would say, "Next responder?" Soon the children began to be more involved, though, and to listen better. Their questions and comments began to be genuinely helpful to the writer. When the writing sounded weird or the plots of their stories were coming unglued, the responders said so. They "praised" without fail.

I remember the group with Yvette, Amy, Henry, and Ngoc. This was a mixed group, though not unusually so. Yvette and Henry were bilingual and both good students from educated families. (Henry spoke Korean at home, and Yvette spoke Czech.)

Amy, the only one born in the United States, was immature—a giggler with a short attention span. She was writing a fairy tale because the boys were. (Yvette's work was about her own experiences in training a pet dog.) Amy had no serious intentions: writing and responding were only play. She loved to praise the others' work but saw little need for encouragement or revision. Although we had talked as a class about describing a character by saying what the character did, Amy did not see any of this as having a connection to her story.

Then one day, Amy began to listen. I could hear her voice on the tape, as though she were hearing something new and wanted to know what it meant. She had just read out her fairy tale, to which Yvette was responding. Yvette has made the comment, "I think you should describe the people, and why did he—"

Amy interrupts, saying quite loudly: "Wait, wait, wait. What do you mean describe the people?"

Then Yvette, with all the patience in the world, says, "Describe the wizard, the mermaid, and Chris."

Then, Amy, suddenly the model student, says, "How should I describe them?"

Yvette is right there with the answer: "Like normal people. Like were they fat, skinny? What's their personalities?"

Then Amy, no longer playing games but instead saying something she really means, comes right back. "That doesn't matter," she says.

"Yes, it does," says Yvette, "so we know what kind of person they are. You could tell what kind of personality they had . . . and . . . ummmm . . . how old was the wizard."

I was amazed, not just at Yvette but at most of the children. How easily they applied these abstract ideas about writing. How seriously they took their responsibility to teach others in their group.

I was particularly interested in following Ngoc, a Vietnamese immigrant. He had arrived in Monterey at the beginning of fourth grade and was placed in my grade four-five class. (Normally, I teach fifth grade, but that year I taught a combination.) He spoke very little English. He could not read or write *any* language. As part of the later wave of Vietnamese refugees—the boat people who came well after the fall of Saigon—his family was poor and had been poor for a long time in Vietnam. His mother now worked all day to support him and his older brothers. I used to hear from the other children that his brothers would play tricks on him and not let him in the house after school. His father apparently was still in Vietnam.

But Ngoc was determined. During fourth-grade reading time he and I read together, and he attended our English-as-a-second-language class for a half hour daily. As soon as he had a rudimentary vocabulary, he joined a writing group as a fifth member. At the beginning, he composed in pictures. He took his drawings to the group meeting, and the group members helped him to convey the message of the picture in written English. He picked up a great deal of English by listening to the others and by joining in as he could. The group members saw by his drawings that his thinking was elaborate, that he was already a person with a language, and that he was in the process of acquiring yet another language—hard things for monolingual children to understand. By fifth grade, his English was good enough for him to become a functioning member of a writing response group. His math was very good, and by the end of fifth grade, he had scored above the eighth-grade level on the CTBS standardized math test (California Test of Basic Skills). Even his language score, 4.8, came close to fifth-grade level.

Ngoc had good relationships with his classmates in the response group. The person he respected most was Henry. The girls—Yvette and Amy—he tolerated, but Henry he listened to and imitated. Henry was male, Asian, and bilingual. He was born in Korea and had been brought to this country as a baby. No doubt Ngoc found it easy to identify with him. But he must also have found it easy to like someone who so obviously listened to his questions and treated them with respect.

Suzie   When Suzanne told me she was taping all these group meetings, I was awestruck at the size of the project she had taken on. I listened to her presentation on response groups at an international conference of English teachers in Ottawa in April 1985, drawn in by her attention to the social and intellectual lives of the children. Then I began to visit her in California and listen to tapes with her. Back home in Hawaii, I transcribed portions of the tapes and spent many hours looking at the language of Ngoc and his group.

Ngoc was an impressive imitator. He had good ears, and made the idiom of the fairy tale his own. Notice the fluency of his fairy tale's first sentence:

> Once upon a time in a small village near the edge of the forest lived Robert and his mother.

This is not a colloquial style of English but the stylized, written language of the storybook. Henry's opening is likewise stylized:

> One day in the forest all the animals were living happily together when some people came with bulldozers and started tearing down the trees to make room for new buildings.

Ngoc has apparently imitated the stories he has heard read aloud in this classroom. He has heard many.

Ngoc has picked up the demands of plot for scary situations, for complicating action, and for a protagonist who accomplishes brave deeds, has feelings, and solves problems in resourceful ways:

> The footsteps came closer and closer until he saw a cow running away from a mean-looking bear. Robert took off his bow and arrow and aimed it right at the bear and felt a little sorry for him but he was a little happy too because he had never hunted a bear before. Robert decided to take the bear and the cow home, so he found some vines and tied the bear on the cow's back.

Not only has Ngoc learned the conventions of English stories, but he has learned as well the verbal routine of the group meeting. The tapes show that he often repeats the phrasing used by the children just before him. His "pointing" phrases are an example. Suzanne has taught the class to "point" to sections of the text that they like, by repeating the phrases and saying why they like them. Yvette says to Ngoc: "I liked that part where the arrow went through the bear's head. That was funny." At his next turn, Ngoc says to Henry, "I like how you say 'kicked out!'" (You can hear him savoring the words.) Yvette says to Henry, "That part where you go, 'what, what, what?' That confused me." Ngoc says to Henry, only slightly less grammatically: "It's confuse me when you go, 'what, what, what.'"

Imitation allows Ngoc the opportunity to join in, to join in immediately, and to do so with a ready flow of language.

However, Ngoc does more than imitate. He asks good questions, which I notice are mainly addressed to Henry. "Why did the king trust the devil?" he asks Henry. "I don't think the king is foolish enough to trust the devil." Why, in other words, would any person in their right mind trust someone whose intentions were so clearly harmful? In my view, this is quite a remarkable question because it brings Ngoc's value system smack into contact with the schoolroom exercise. He gives the exercise human sense.

Henry apparently sees the point in what Ngoc has said about the possible inconsistency of the character he has created. "Okay," he replies. "It was too easy for the devil."

Ngoc asks enough questions of this general type over the course of several meetings to convince me that the first one is not a lucky accident but an internalized pattern of thinking. He asks, "Why didn't she hire a detective?" He asks, "Why are the people tearing down the forest? Why did the animals leave the forest? Why didn't they stay and fight?" He says, "I think if you put that, you should have a reason."

Ngoc consistently pits the events of the story against his own sense of what's likely to happen. Luckily for him, the group structure makes a place and a time for him to raise his logical questions and express the values that lie behind these questions. Not only is he learning that questioning is a conventional form of expressing values, but he is also learning the tone of near contentiousness that we

Westerners find appropriate. He has acquired this elaborate range of verbal arts in a little over a year and a half.

Suzanne
....

Without the tapes I never would have known about Ngoc's growing ability to ask good questions. For one thing, he never said these wonderful things in large-group discussion, so I didn't hear them. For another, when I read his stories and other writings, I saw no evidence that he was thinking logically about revision. In this particular story I saw only a rambling account of Robert and some other main characters, including a cat named Forval and a father who resembled someone in an American television sitcom. In the end, his story turned into a beautifully illustrated manuscript of thirty-five pages, which he published at the end of the year as his "book." (Almost every child publishes a book of poems, or an autobiography, or a story.) Ngoc was proud of his effort, though he didn't see that shorter might have been more powerful.

Yvette tried her hardest to get him to cut, giving him the perfect piece of advice. "Add a dragon," she said, "but shorten the story." Suzie and I talked about her advice, deciding that writers could improve practically any piece of writing by adding a dragon. In a later meeting, she tried again, with great explicitness, to say *how* to add a dragon:

> Somewhere in the story you should say, like on page seventeen you should say, umm, that *Forval and Robert one day went to the forest and couldn't find anything to kill for dinner, so they went farther in the forest when they ran into this castle guarded by a seven-headed dragon* (or as many heads as you want). *Then they kill the dragon and save the maiden and live happily ever after, the cat in the castle.* How does that sound? You should, like, just make anything to make some more exciting. Like they have THIS BIG FIGHT, you know, and they're all BLEEDING and they have CUTS and everything.

But not this piece of advice, nor even Yvette's remark, "Ngoc! you didn't change a thing," had any effect whatsoever. Ngoc loved his story and was not about to change any of it. I could have concluded from his finished story that he did not understand how to think about revision, but I would have been far off the mark. Luckily for me, I had the tapes to show how far he had come in his ability to think critically.

<u>Suzie</u>   Some teachers feel that every piece of writing must be revised, or that all good pieces will necessarily be revised pieces, or that response groups must be evaluated entirely by the quality of the revisions that follow. Suzanne deliberately heightens children's consciousness of themselves as people who use response for the purpose of revision, but as she and I studied these tapes and transcripts, we concluded that the response-group dialogue had an effect not seen in the revisions alone. We saw that effect in the increasingly sophisticated dialogue. The tapes show that the peer-group discussions can stand on their own merits, whether revision follows or not. I found that the groups encouraged serious, group-supported thought. I often thought that the children were more thoughtful in their group talk than in their writing. I heard "critical thinking."

John McPeck has defined critical thinking as "healthy skepticism" (1981, 6–7). Back to Descartes and beyond, Western philosophers have urged us to doubt: to question the evidence of our senses, to suspect the validity of our conclusions, and to wonder whether our words might deceive. When I looked at tapes of another group, I saw that the children were *doubting*. They puzzled; they wondered; they asked about the meanings of words, and over all conveyed a tone of friendly skepticism (see Figure 6–1). "Are you *sure* about that? Could it be some other way?"

All this intense cogitation took place in the context of a science assignment. Suzanne said that she normally would not ask ten-year-olds to select a newspaper article about an environmental problem and to write about the problem and its possible solution. But that year she did. The children had just spent a week in science camp in the mountains, where they talked about the environment all day long, every day. They seemed ready for this.

Pro's Side

The Sceintists, USA and others nations want to reduce the use of CFC's 90 percent so we can save the layer of Ozone, this means if we ban it 90 percent then we can't use compuiters, refrigrants, the chemicals in firefighting and foams as much as we do now.

What I think about the Problem

I think they should ban CFC's but only 70 percent because we use the things that have CFC's in it. I don't want the ozone layer to be destroyed so skin cancer can increase but the things that have CFC's in them are very important to us.

By Erika

FIGURE 6-1   Erika's Writing for Thinking (Unedited): "The Pro Side" and "What I Think About the Problem"

Larry perhaps got in over his head, having selected the green-house effect as his problem. In several lengthy discussions of his paper, the three other children—Erika, Jenny and Anastassis—asked questions he couldn't answer. What's this about "chlorofluorocarbons"? Why should a change in climate cause skin cancer? Why should it harm sea life? Are you sure you know what ozone does? I have excerpted a piece of this discussion (see Figure 6–2).

At the beginning, having just read out his writing, Larry answers as though the facts about ozone, the sun, and the climate were all obvious. "No, no, no," he says impatiently. But as the other children keep on with their questions, he stops to consider. "Well, maybe . . ." he says. From this point forward, he's not so quick to answer.

Larry has the wrong idea of the greenhouse effect. He believes the greenhouse to be a positive thing, a shelter, instead of something ominous that will overheat the earth. He thinks that the greenhouse has been there all along, protecting the earth, and now something is wrong: someone has broken the windows of the greenhouse. As he attempts to answer the question "Why is the house called greenhouse?" he tries to say why the damage to the ozone layer is like broken windows in the greenhouse. But his interpretation isn't working. He pauses repeatedly, clears his throat, starts again, and finally puts the question to himself: "How is that?" At this point, having tried to explain, he knows there's something he doesn't know.

Larry's next attempt at speculation—about fish, rising water, and chemicals—doesn't quite make sense either. But the long, slow "hmmmmmmmm" at the end of the excerpt seems full of potential. Doubting is a way to think further, to open up a closed subject.

Larry and his writing group: Larry journeys from certainty to doubt. (Dash indicates a child speaker other than Larry.)

    Larry [reading his paper]: The problem is that all the air pollution is ruining the atmosphere. And bad things could

Continued on page 96

happen. The climate could change. A lot of people could get skin cancer, and it could hurt sea life. The sun's rays could break the earth's layer of ozone which protects the earth.

—What does the ozone layer protect the earth from?

Larry [as if obvious]: It protects it from the sun's rays.

—And who is dealing with this problem and where?

Larry: The earth. The whole earth is dealing with the problem.

—Didn't this . . . didn't the whole earth . . .

Larry: No, no, no.

—get sun stuff? I mean isn't scientists or somebody looking at this problem to see how to solve it or something?

Larry [with insistence]: They all are!

—Everybody is, right?

Larry: Everybody, yes!

—OK. Is there one main person or a group of people who are pursuing the [unclear] to this problem?

Larry: I don't think so. Well, maybe scientists. [pause]

—OK, you should explain what ozone is.

Larry: It's, it's—to protect . . . what protects the earth from the sun's rays, but—[as if to self] that's what I said in here. Well, wait, let me see.

—You said that . . . you just said that the sun's rays could break the layer of ozone.

Larry: Yeah! well . . . when . . . when the, ahhh . . the climate gets too hot, uh, wait.

—You mean when it gets hot . . .

Larry: Yeah! [as if to say, "That's it!"] The sun, like, gets too close. From all the pollution.

—Why is the . . . is the house called greenhouse?

Larry: Because the . . . the greenhouse, hmmm [clears throat] . . . the green [clears throat again]. The article's called "The Greenhouse Effect," but because . . . like, the o— . . . the layer of ozone is like the . . . the windows on a greenhouse. How is that? And like if it broke the windows or something, then . . .

—OK. And why could [it] hurt sea life, the sea life?

Continued on page 97

Larry: Because, like, uh, [clears throat] if that happened, the ummm water could rise, like about four inches, and all the [clears throat] some of the . . . uh, sea life could like wash up onto the land or something, or all the, all the, the sun could get too hot and the water too hot or something, and like if the fish or something swam, it would be covering houses and stuff, so there could be some chemicals and stuff that get into the water. Hmmmmmmmm [softly].

FIGURE 6–2   Transcript of a Small Group Meeting

Suzanne   As it happened, many of Larry's questions about ozone never got answered that year. He thought the holes in the ozone layer were made by the sun, as though the sun had broken the windows, rather than by chemicals released into the atmosphere. Erika said to him once, "The sun doesn't make holes in the ozone." But he held this vision of the sun as the culprit strongly, and of course I didn't catch on to this misconception until much later, when I sat down and listened to these tapes a second time. The whole process heightened his curiosity, and he probably answered all these questions later on, but not in fifth grade. When he revised his writing, he chose to ignore several of the science questions and concentrated instead on the human question. "One side of the problem," he wrote, "is that some people think that this is not a big problem right now. They think that they should deal with it later, when it's closer to happening. They're not worried."

Suzie   Larry has made strides toward being an interested and curious thinker. The fact that he chooses to comment on people's perception of the problem—whether they are worried or not—is evidence of a growing ability to analyze. The fact that he misinterprets the facts is less significant than his willingness to forge ahead and take risks. When I look at Larry's language—at the language of Ngoc, Henry,

Yvette, and even Amy—I see intellectual curiosity that will stay with these children long past fifth grade. I see them as people who will sit in my university classroom down the line, and when that happens, I'll praise the day.

Suzanne
. . . .

For children to run their own groups is risky. They risk getting the facts wrong, as Larry did, and they face other risks as well. Teachers express to me three kinds of reservations about having their children meet without them. They say, "This is just too hard" and the children "can't do it." Or they say that the children won't stay "on task"—that they will simply use the time for "idle chatter." Or they say that the groups will have the kind of problems Elizabeth Cohen (1986) described: They'll fall apart, be dysfunctional. The children won't take turns, and they won't help each other.

When teachers say, "It's just too hard," I think they're talking about how rough it is to get started and how shallow some of the early meetings are. I agree with their views of these meetings, but I don't see the shallowness as failure, only part of getting started. As for "idle chatter," isn't this what adults do when they get together in groups? I heard a fair amount of idle chatter on the tapes, but I judged the groups in terms of what they accomplished over the long haul. I didn't measure the time on task.

As for "falling apart," I've had groups do this. Though I held my breath and wondered momentarily whether the groups were really worth the trouble, I decided in the end that their worth had to be measured not in terms of falling apart but in terms of pulling themselves back together. Let me explain.

The year that I taped every group meeting, things fell apart. In February, after three months of meetings, something in the atmosphere changed. This was more than a minor squabble. This was grumbling on a large scale. The rains that were supposed to end by mid-February had not ended. For whatever reason, tempers grew short.

"Fred's spoiling our group," said Maryann. "He throws paper, and tips back in his chair. He fools around."

"Maryann's too bossy. She's always telling me what to do, interrupting."

Amy couldn't stop giggling. The chairpersons tried, but they couldn't enforce the rules. This was serious. I called a halt to the group meetings.

"You mean no more response groups?"

"Maybe not."

For a couple of weeks they did not meet. "Who will I talk to for response?" they asked.

"Well," I said, "just read to the person next to you."

"But that's not as good. That person doesn't know my work and I'll have to start all over. Besides, *our* group was good, and we have to meet."

I waited until I heard a little begging. Then I said, "What will we do?"

"We have to have a big meeting," said one. The rest agreed.

At this point, I organized a full-class, problem-solving session, making this a highly organized affair. First, I wanted to make sure that I heard from every child and that their comments could be anonymous. Second, I wanted everyone to consider everyone else's comments. Third, I wanted the children to suggest solutions and negotiate.

What was the problem in their group? What good things were happening there? Could they name one change that would make their group go better?

I had all the children write their answers, without names, and hand them to me. I read out a summary of the answers, which showed that every child in the class thought that the groups were necessary and wanted to have the meetings again. Apparently, the children had forgotten the distracting behavior. The single nuisance, which was mentioned by a number of children, was the tape recorder itself. Some children played with the buttons, and others thought they shouldn't.

Then came the large-group discussion, which surprised me by its length. The children's talk went on and on, right through recess. Finally, I said *enough*. What were they going to do?

I consented to their idea that group members should be able to switch to new groups as long as they could arrange a trade. Ordinarily I insist that writing response groups stay together all year long, but this time I said OK. Three people changed groups, not including Fred or Maryann. Apparently, the large-group discussion worked magic. The air immediately cleared, and we were back in business for the rest of the year. No groups have fallen apart since.

Now I pay close attention to complaints, to the sources of unease or confusion. Roger was right about strictly enforcing the rules of procedure. During the first few group meetings, I walk around to see that chairs are in the specified positions, everyone has brought extra paper and a pencil, everyone has something to read, turns are being taken in order, everyone is reading twice, and the tone is friendly and helpful. I'm modeling the chairperson's responsibilities. After that, I meet with the chairpersons regularly. Groups relax the rules after a while, making them the group's own version of what works, and that's fine unless a problem crops up.

"John keeps talking to Mike. He doesn't pay attention to our group," one of the chairpersons tells me. John has moved his chair back, turned it around, and now leans over the back. He's broken the invisible "tent of purpose" that surrounds a tight group. He's open to distraction. He also has no lap for his response paper. I ask the chairperson to remind him of the rules.

"Julie doesn't give any responses except to say what other kids say." Julie hasn't remembered to bring paper or pencil. Remind her of the rules.

"Jamie argues with everybody." Remind him of the rules.

In large-group discussion, I have the children talk about what kinds of responses are helping and ask them to talk about why they should have rules for the groups. The problems are handled by the chairperson with my charge to remember the rules.

Another kind of problem is reflected in the complaint "Andy isn't bringing any writing to read, and it's not because he's working on a final draft." During the next writing workshop, Andy and I discuss his writing goals folder. This is a loose collection of papers on which Andy keeps a daily record of what he plans to do during the writing

What I Plan to do	What I Did
3/8 Work on conversation of mother & Alissa	Did that, wrote 2 pages got a drink, helped Beth think of a tittle
3/9 Meet with group	met with group
3/10 go on with my story	met with Tim to proofread his story wrote 4 pages
3/11 Meet with group	met with group
3/15 change some of my story	changed it, helped Beth
3/16 Meet with group	met with group
3/17 finish story	all most finished
3/18 Meet with group	met with group
3/ add more	wrote 4 pages

FIGURE 6–3   A Page from the Writing Goals Folder

hour and what he actually did (see Figure 6–3). Whatever is keeping Andy from generating ideas, or drafting, can be addressed by the two of us.

So now I can face problems as they occur by saying, "Remember the rules and let's look at your goals folder." When the groups came to a halt, it spurred me to find better ways of helping the children identify then solve their group's problems.

Looking back at that year, I sometimes reflect on the large-group meeting where things got hashed out. I think the success of that meeting was not an accident. At that point in the year, the group meeting process was so well rehearsed that I felt there was little else I had to do than call the meeting and ensure that everyone participated by writing answers to questions. Back in September and October I had led the children to work together as writers in groups. This was the object of the scaffolding described in chapter 5. But now we had come full circle. Response had become a means by which the children could reconsider their working relationships—indeed, reconsider the whole social and emotional climate of the classroom. I was reminded again, and so were they, that intelligence is multiple. Social intelligence is both cause and effect of academic learning.

How effective, then, were the writing response groups? They did not always hang together. They were no insurance against error. And they did not always lead to good revisions of written products (though they often did). But every child who has been in a child-led writing group in my classroom has learned to carry on a conversation about writing with the reader in mind. All of these children have finished the year with an enriched sense of themselves as social beings, as people who see that writing is a natural thing to do and to talk about.

One last aspect of evaluation is the children's grade, which for many of us who teach writing is the ultimate teaching dilemma. Each year I ask the children to think of themselves as real writers. But then come report cards, and grades, and the teacher as evaluator. On the quarterly report card, I grade only effort, which is either "good" or "very good." The children, the parents, and I are all comfortable with that. At the end of the year, the children gather all of

Doing response groups has really helped me and my stories and the other pupils in my response group. I plan to write my new story 'Anna's Tutor' to be as long as it possibly can, even if it means I'll have to write during the summer. I have plans for that story that I personaly think it's pretty good. The only problem is that Room 11 won't be able to hear it.

And I think that my strength as a writer is to imagine things and write them down, in other words I'm a good author.

Last year I was not a very good writer. I was ofull. But this year I have made a inproonand. And not Just on my stories, on my hand writing.

My grade is very hard to give my self so I take in friends comments and all the things I have acomplished I give my self the grade A, with the recomindashen of Marianne.

FIGURE 6–4 Children's Evaluation of Their Work in Writing (Unedited)

their published pieces together in a final portfolio and write me letters about themselves as writers (see Figure 6–4). They also write a letter about their response group. I ask them to look at what they've accomplished, how they've stretched and grown, and in the context of our community of writers, to give themselves a grade. Letter grades—*A*, *B*, and *C*—used to be difficult for them to think about. Now, with a new report card and a range from "needs improvement" to "excellent," they more easily find an appropriate word of self-evaluation. Rarely do I disagree with their conclusions.

SEVEN

Changing the Way We Teach Reading

Suzie "How do you do classroom reading?" I asked Suzanne. I was all innocence. It had been a fairly straightforward matter to bring her writing instruction into line with her ideas about children as social beings. She saw the need for change and a way to make it. Now I expected to hear about the social approach to reading. What did she do and why? How did she innovate?

But when I first asked Suzanne about her reading program, she was subdued. "We use a basal reader," she said. I could tell she didn't want to talk about it.

In the 1970s, basal reading programs came in for scathing criticism. While the public saw only the screaming headlines ("Why

Can't Johnny Read?"), critics in school circles complained, "Why don't reading programs *encourage* reading?" As far back as the 1960s, university professor Ken Goodman had begun to argue that basal reading programs spent too much time on word-attack skills and not enough on getting children to think about the piece of reading as a whole (1965).

Attacks on the basal readers came from the media, teacher organizations, and universities. Basal reading systems were pseudoscientific. The breakdown of reading into many subskills was not a valid teaching approach. The workbooks were busy work. Children were so busy filling in blanks that they had little time to read. There was too much phonics at the higher grade levels. There was too much testing. The teacher's manual insulted the intelligence of teachers.

Coming in for the sharpest criticism was the general quality of the reading material and the practice of including only excerpts of books, omitting parts that described the setting or characters. Publishers rewrote books to simplify the vocabulary. They shortened the sentences and sometimes cut out metaphor (Goodman, et al. 1988; Smith 1986). Some critics wondered why school authorities couldn't purchase trade books in their full versions instead of the basals with cut versions. Trade books were less expensive.[1]

But basal reading systems had remarkable staying power. It was easy to fit the components—the daily exercise sheets and the skills tests—into the daily schedule. It was easy to show the children's hopefully steady progress up the charts of subskills (termed *scope and sequence* charts) because they demonstrated to everybody—the curriculum supervisor, the teacher, the parent, and the child—the direction in which learning should proceed. The sequenced workbooks made it clear how to provide for children of differing abilities: the low groups spent their time on basic skills, while the higher groups answered thought questions. Since the teachers met with each group, their time was planned for them. Since the manual set out the questions for them to ask, they knew what to do, and administrators knew that they knew. The frequent tests rounded out the system: since workbook skills were prominent in the tests, it was easy for the administrator to be sure that teachers used the workbook. In sum, the components of the system fit the culture of the school, leaving little room for surprise and ensuring tight control of curriculum by administrators.

Tracy Kidder's best-seller *Among Schoolchildren* (1989) shows fifth-grade teacher Chris Zajac struggling with a traditional basal system. Kidder makes the point that the system is "brand new." It's obviously expensive.

> They were more than reading books. They were mountains of equipment: big charts for teaching what were called "skill lessons," and big metal frames to hold the charts erect, and workbooks for the children to practice those skills. . . . (29)

The children, says Kidder, hated the workbooks. The ones with the worst skills, portrayed by Kidder as "slumped over those workbooks," hated them most. Even Judith, the best reader in the class, hated the workbooks. For her there was a sharp distinction between real reading and doing the reading program. "I love reading," she said, "but I hate reading reading."

Kidder's tone is incredulous when he describes the teacher's manual:

> . . . a fat teacher's manual that went so far as to print out in boldface type the very words that Chris, or any other teacher anywhere, should say to her pupils, so as to *make* them learn to read. (29)

The teacher, Chris Zajac, felt many of the same pressures that Suzanne felt in the years just after I met her. She couldn't quit the basal, but she wanted her ten-year-old children to feel that there was more to reading than the workbook. She wanted them to enrich themselves by reading, to learn to enjoy it, and to have some choice in what they read. With great effort Chris managed to squeeze twenty-five minutes out of the reading program each day for free-choice reading. "Read whatever you like," she said. She wished she had children's novels available and wondered if an administrator could help her find some.

Teachers like Suzanne urged their children to buy books, to go to the library, and to read at home. Many took time to read aloud in school. But in the end none of this reading counted as learning activity. It was called "reading for pleasure" or "outside reading." It wasn't "learning to read."

"Learning to read" took hours every day. Suzanne sometimes had as many as seven different ability levels, so she had to meet with seven groups. Some teachers would save time by trading children with other teachers at reading time. They'd say, "I have three in *Golden Secrets,*" which was one of the workbook levels. "How many do you have? Why don't you take my three, and I'll take your three who are in *Sea Treasures*" (*Scott Foresman Reading Series* 1983). So they'd do a trade. But Suzanne, wanting to stay in touch with every child's reading, didn't want to economize this way.

Each group meeting took time. To teach as the basal program wanted her to teach, Suzanne had to first present vocabulary. She had to supply the setting and describe the characters; she had to spend time putting back the details that the publishers had stripped away from the original work to make the reading excerpts short enough. Then she had the group begin reading, which was mainly a process of answering comprehension questions. The teacher's manual often advised having the children read silently until they found the answer to a question, something like: "Read to find out what happens to Bill when he goes to the auto show and when you find out, raise your hand." So the group limped through the chapter like this, stopping and starting. When the children got to the end, there were more questions, which might be: "What did Bill learn at the auto show? Tell why you think Grandma does not want to move with the family." The manual, which told the teacher precisely what to do, was enormously comforting.

For Suzanne, it was impossible to meet with every group each day. For the children not meeting with her, she prepared seat work to keep them busy and quiet. She was grateful to the reading series for their worksheets. Otherwise, she had no hope of teaching the groups without interruption. If she could have left the groups to work on their own, then the individualized seat work would not have been necessary. But she couldn't have the groups meeting without her because the context setting and the presentation of vocabulary could not be carried out by the children. She had to be there. Consequently, she was in a race with the clock all day.

Change came. It came for Suzanne, it came for her district, and it came to many classrooms that had formerly used the traditional basal. The theme of the change was "learn to read by reading literature," not excerpted pieces but whole works of literature. The word *whole* in this phrase echoed the larger theme, "whole language," which came to be an influential movement in language arts circles in Canada, the United States, and indeed the English-speaking world.

Whole language was largely a set of shared assumptions about what was wrong with past practice. Whole language proponents liked neither the skills approach to reading, nor the drill and practice approach to writing, nor the workbooks and tests that went along with these approaches. All of these fragmented the normal process of reading. It was known from the experience of the new curriculum in writing that children could write whole pieces, whole stories and arguments, and in fact whole books. They could surely read whole works of literature as well. A corollary notion was that writing and reading, being parts of a whole, should be joined together instead of artificially broken apart in different time blocks of the school day.

How to do whole language in the classroom, however, was something of a mystery. Whole language teachers did different things but used the same label, *whole language,* to apply to them. Some districts that were committed to whole language, such as Suzanne's, went along with modified basal programs. Other districts followed the trend toward "reading as literature" by dispensing with textbooks altogether. They began to buy trade books such as Katherine Paterson's *Bridge to Terabithia* (1987)—whole sets so that everyone in the class had copies. Practice varied depending on the district and sometimes the school or the individual teacher. Talk to textbook publishers nowadays, and they'll tell you that educators should get together and make up their minds what whole language is; then they could publish books that fit this definition.

The meaning of whole language is clearest for the faction that has dispensed with textbooks altogether, the reading-as-literary-study group. These people are guided by their common experience as students in English departments. They regard the book as an object of value, worth appreciating. As they talk, they use words such as *theme* and *plot,* and they expect students to use this vocabulary too. They wish to keep the study of the book separate from what they regard as low-level skills such as spelling. They value discussion and analysis, so they have students use writing to discuss and analyze the works of literature.

These practices have been in place for many years in college and high school. Increasingly, they have made their way into middle schools. Now, in some districts, teachers at the elementary school level are getting together to prepare packets of materials—"units"—so as to bring literary study into the fourth and fifth grades.

Larger by far than the reading-as-literary-study group is the group of whole language people who have stayed with basal programs. To call these people a group may be a misnomer. It's clear, looking at the array of basals designed for whole language, that the publishers have attempted to reach a cross section of educators: those intent on skills, those who want literary study, and those in the middle who think that both sides have merit.

The new whole language basals have corrected the most blatant faults of the old-style programs. The new teacher's manuals are less inclined to be scripted, more inclined to include suggestions from which the teacher should choose. Large-group discussion, not just the traditional homogeneous small-group circle, is encouraged. The workbooks have less drill and practice, more space for writing assignments, and more attention to thinking rather than searching the text for the right answer. Most of the skills tests are now gone. In some cases, trade books are now included as part of the basal package. There's a little something for everybody.

In California, state educational authorities have laid down guidelines for approving the purchase of basal textbooks in the state (Barr 1988). To meet the state's approval, the publishers

1. must not *rewrite* the selections, but instead must use the original author's language

2. must use only exercises and assignments linked with the reading, not unrelated skill drills

3. must require no ability grouping

It remains to be seen how eagerly district administrators will take up the new basal systems. The traditional basal programs had staying power because they fit the culture of the school. The explicit, scripted teacher's manual was particularly appropriate. The new manuals, with only a "suggestion" format, may prove to be unsuited to the school's hierarchical organization. The workbook pages, with only lines to be filled in, may inspire the question, "Why not buy blank composition books instead?" The role of the whole language basals within the structure and culture of the school is not very clear; the role of the teacher within the new basal systems is hard to define.

The second type of whole language program, the reading-as-literary-study type, may be different because the role of the teacher has a long history. This role is well known to teachers schooled in the culture of university English departments. The role continues to be played in high school and sometimes middle school. In spite of the fact that it discourages children from asking real questions, it may have gained a foothold in the elementary school because of its long-standing academic tradition.

Is it possible to invent a new and different cultural pattern for classroom reading in the upper elementary grades? One would hope so.

Suzanne   I knew I wanted to change from the old basal program. I was troubled when year after year, in a school with good teachers, interested parents, and a fine library and librarian, I had too many students who read words but didn't really read. I was supposed to feel lucky that half or more of my students could read at grade level or above, but I saw that only a few of these children loved to read. In a world where children spend their time with television, home video games, and organized sports, only a very few kept a book at home by their bed. Half to two-thirds of the children in the class read competently enough, finished their workbook pages, and saw reading as a piece of their school life. But no more than that.

A third entered the class reading below grade level. A few of this third were diagnosed as having learning problems and were assigned to the resource program, but most had no diagnosable problem. These children just found reading painful and a chore. "I hate reading," they'd confide—and break my heart. They could sound out words reasonably well. The primary grades emphasized phonics, and in the early grades, their scores on tests, which emphasized decoding, were at grade level. But as they grew older, their test scores, which increasingly were based on comprehension, lagged farther and farther behind the grade norm. They loved to hear me read every day after lunch, but in their own reading time they sighed with resignation. At some earlier point they had "tried harder," but it was all for naught. Reading for pleasure had no place in their lives.

What could I do about this? Give them more interesting reading? Maybe so. Marilyn said to me, "Suzanne, this is awful. Look at the wonderful things they're writing, and look at the stuff we give them to read." More interesting reading might be the nudge needed by the more competent readers, but what about the readers still reading word for word? These children were playing the notes on the musical score but not listening to the music. They were not comprehending. An ordinary children's novel with chapters—let's say *Where the Red Fern Grows* (Rawls 1974)—was out of reach. I might as well have asked them to read a nineteenth-century novel.

I was determined to confront the basal program, remove it, and put real reading in its place. I waited until I saw that the writing program was fully on its feet, gathered up my energy, and, applying what I had learned as I changed the writing program earlier, began to plan.

I decided to ignore the district's new basals. The children needed to read whole books. I started from that point.

The children also needed choice. Because they selected topics for writing, they had established ownership over their writing. They needed to select what to read as well. This was selection that assumed a community of readers, a group of people reading the same book. I remembered the days when choosing your own book meant going off to read it by yourself, then having a miniconference with the teacher so that you could be quizzed on what you were reading. This remnant of traditional classroom culture was not what I wanted.

I knew I needed writing but certainly not book reports, which I saw as devices to prove to the teacher that the book had been read.

Book report writing was too often formulaic and its purpose more a test than an appreciation of author or text. I needed writing that was more personal, more expressive.

I knew that I needed groups. I knew that these should be mixed in ability, like the writing response groups. And I knew that I had to stay out of them. Being responsible for helping and teaching others had to be part of the children's consciousness. If I were in the group, the children would put me in charge and make me responsible.

I knew that the children would have to be coached in their roles. Key to learning was conversation, the dialogue that readers customarily use when they talk about their books with other readers. Silence was not golden; the yes-no response style of the IRE sequence was not what I wanted in the groups.

Dialogue was crucial. I began to think, "As I read, what do I do?" It was so simple. When reading, I talked to myself. I thought, "Well, I need to tell the children that's what readers do." Of course, I knew it wasn't as simple as telling them. I'd been telling children for years that they had to read with their brains and not just their eyes, but many truly read with their eyes only. I used to say to children in the primary grades, "When you get to the end of the passage and it says, 'How many legs did Mrs. Goat have?', the good reader will say, 'Six, and when I read it, I wondered about that.' The poor reader," I would tell them, "will say, 'Legs? Mrs. Goat?', and go back and read the whole passage again."

Now the rather mysterious process of making sense of what is read seemed simpler than before. Children needed to talk to themselves while reading—to wonder, to puzzle, to react. Good readers think when they read.

I wanted the reading program to change, but the main question—how to get them to think—was not entirely answered. I was nervous about not being able to hear each child. Might some of the children slide? Might some get into difficulties that I would discover too late? Even if I didn't sit in on the groups, I wanted to hear the thinking of each child so that I didn't lose anybody.

What was missing was a scaffold. If I didn't sit in and lead the groups, I had no vehicle to get them started. Neither did they have a vehicle to show me that they had gotten the idea.

Just at the time I was debating how to build a scaffold, a conference came up. With our mentor budgets Marilyn and I got substitutes and headed for an NCTE meeting in Los Angeles. I was looking for help, but I didn't expect anything extraordinary to happen. I really had no idea that I'd have another one of those moments like the one on Maui when Suzie said "chaos" and my chair jumped. This time the presenters were a group of teachers from Virginia—third-grade, eighth-grade, and university teachers—who had done a joint project in a writing project institute (Glaze, et al. 1987).

Their project was to investigate the use of response logs as an alternative to comprehension questions. They passed out sample logs that had been written by students at all three levels. Among these, for example, was a third grader's response to *The Trumpet of the Swan* (White 1973), which read like a running diary of the child's thoughts while he read. I nudged Marilyn, who was sitting beside me. "Look at this," I said. The teachers stood at the front showing one response log after another. Each log was as different as its writer, but all of them engaged with the people, the situations, and the feelings of the book. "Every child in our classes, at every grade level, could do this," the presenters said.

"Marilyn!" I wanted to say, "Yoo-hoo! Did you hear what they said? Marilyn, *we* could do this." We went back to the hotel, and I'm sure I didn't stop talking for hours and hours. The response log was an important piece of the scaffold that we needed to build. It would serve as a conversation, or rather the step the children needed to enter into the conversation. At the same time, the log would keep me in touch with every child. If someone was getting lost, I'd know.

Because the conference was held in the spring, Marilyn and I had all summer to plan for a different reading program in September. We gave up the basal reader. We started using whole books, children's novels. We stopped doing vocabulary presentation and context setting. We quit doing the publisher's comprehension questions, and we stopped having teacher-led reading circles. What we began to do was to create a social routine that put children's questions first. This routine is described in detail in chapter 8.

One footnote is that we didn't stop using the workbooks, not right away. For one thing, the school's reading resource teacher kept a file in her office of every child's scores on the tests of subskills. Every once in a while I'd have the children race through a few workbook pages and do the tests so that I'd have scores to turn in. After a while, I said to myself, "This is not necessary." I had other ways of teaching spelling, punctuation, and the other mechanics of writing. I took courage and said to the school administration, "I've stopped using the basal, and this year we won't need the workbooks either." The workbooks were the last thing to go.

NOTE

1. For a proponent's view of basal readers, see Robert C. Aukerman (1981, 6): "The teacher's lesson plans [located in the manual] are at the heart of every basal reader series, for they detail the scope and sequence of the reading skills that are to be taught daily at each grade in the elementary school.

"Pupil workbooks are also an essential component of every basal reader series, for it is in the workbooks . . . that the skills are reinforced through practice on exercises.

". . . the tests are used for the purpose of placing pupils in the proper levels of the program, or for identifying certain skills that each pupil needs to acquire or strengthen. The testing also will determine mastery of skills sufficient to allow the pupil to move on to the next higher level." (S. Jacobs)

EIGHT

Good Readers Think While They Read

Suzanne When I begin the reading program, on one of the first days of school, I ask the children to tell me the difference between a good reader and a not-so-good reader. They answer with comments such as "a bad reader is in the low reading group," or "readers can sound out words," or "good readers read for fun." They don't want to say that "bad readers are dumb"—they know there are bad readers in the class—but they do say that "good readers are smart." The inference is that bad readers are not smart.

I'll say, "How do you suppose good readers get to be good? Do you think people just decide that? Is it really hard, once you're in a low reading group, to be put in the highest reading group?" Some of the children nod, not only the people who've been in the low reading groups but also those who have been sent to the lower grades to read. They've got these looks on their faces that seem to say, "It's hopeless. Once you're in a low reading group, you pretty much stay there." They'll identify themselves, when you speak with them one-to-one, as "nine o'clockers." They're aware of the unwritten law that slow groups go earlier in the day, when slow readers supposedly are more mentally alert, and good readers go later in the day. Even as early as first grade, they know where they stand.

So I say, "There's a secret about all this. The secret is that people in the top reading group *think* when they read." (This is news to many. I can see them tuning in.) "And the kids in the low reading group don't know they're supposed to."

Like *intelligent*, the word *think* carries none of the baggage of *smart* or *comprehend*. It's a good word.

"How do people learn to do this?" I ask. "It's kind of a mystery, but some children, even before they can read, have been thinking as they listened to somebody else read: 'Oooh, I wonder how that bad wolf is going to hide himself behind that tree so that Little Red Riding Hood doesn't see him as she walks by.' That sort of thing. By the time they get to the first grade, when they start to learn what the letters mean, they still think, 'Wait a minute. I have to figure this out so it makes sense.'"

"This year," I say, "you'll be learning to think as you read."

At this point, I begin to teach the language of reading, by which I mean the language that readers use when they think and converse about books. Such language is one of the dialogue styles we referred to earlier, a style of language invented at some point in human history and passed down through generations of book readers.

As with writing, I scaffold the children's understanding by returning frequently to key phrases—in this case, "think while you read"—and by setting up social routines of the type that real readers follow:

- choosing a book
- writing in a response log while reading the book

- meeting in a book group with other people who are reading the same book (from three to six people read the same book at the same time)
- writing a book review for people who haven't read the book
- discussing the book with people who haven't read it—in this case, the rest of the class—which I call the "discussion on the rug"
- putting the book out for others to borrow—in this case, by putting it on the metal spinning rack

A book cycle, which is the time it takes the class to go through these routines for a single book such as Armstrong's *Sounder* (1972) or Cleary's *Dear Mr. Henshaw* (1984), is about four weeks. This book is read entirely in school.

This is my reading program, which takes an hour each day. I do no other instruction in reading: no workbooks, no comprehension exercises, no skills tests, and no answers to publishers' or teacher questions. Children do other reading, borrowing books for homework, while they're going through a book cycle in school.

I will explain each of the routines in turn, describing the children's social roles and my role, beginning with choosing a book.

On the first day, I point to the books on the round table at the back of the classroom. There I have sets of five or six each of such books as *Ramona Forever* (Cleary 1985) and *Indian in the Cupboard* (Banks 1985). "You'll be choosing a book," I say, "then you'll read it during reading time in school. Each day you'll write your thoughts in your response log." I show them the kind of spiral notebook they'll be using. "Then you'll meet once or twice a week with your book group, which will include the people who choose the same book that you choose. In the group meeting you'll learn from the others what they thought. You'll help each other learn how to do the thinking."

The choosing routine is rather elaborate, occupying reading periods for two days. Over the course of the school year, these days come to be anxiously awaited; each team wants first crack at the new books.

I begin the routine by gathering the class together and pointing to five or six small piles of books in front of me, which, by the way, must be sure winners if this is the first book cycle of the year. I also put out more copies than there are children so that the last children called to the round table will have more than a single choice.

Then I repeat the point I've made earlier: "People in your book group won't be there because of the level of the book but because they want to read the same book. Each of you will choose a book," I say, "because it's a book you want to read, not because it's easy, not because it's hard, and not because I said this is a book for you. One more thing: It must be a book you haven't read or have had read to you before. Your book group will be upset if you know what's going to happen and how the book ends."

Then I say a very little about each book so that when the children go to the table they'll know which one to pick up first. I hold up *Ramona Forever* and say "This is one of the series by Beverly Cleary, and this is the end of the series." I continue until I have mentioned each of the books.

> *Sounder* (Armstrong 1972): This is about a boy and his dog, a story about the family and the difficult times they had.
>
> *Hatchet* (Paulsen 1988): This is about a boy in the wilderness.
>
> *Number the Stars* (Lowry 1990): This takes place during World War II. It's about a girl and her friend, and problems caused by the war.

Making a choice is both exciting and serious. The children must learn how to think about whether they like the books or not. Once a child has a book in hand, I say, "Take the book to your desk, look it over, and start to read the first chapter. You won't commit to the book until you've read some of it."

On the second morning, the choosing continues. At the same time, I get the children started on the book. "I'd like to see the *Sounder* group on the rug," I'll say. Then I get the group to predict what the book will be about. For the first day or two the children can switch books. For example, they may find they don't want to be stuck with a book in spite of the fact that their best friend, Eddie, is in the group. "There's no bailing out halfway through," I say. "Once you've signed your name on the clipboard under the title of a book, that's your book."

Next comes writing in the response log, which the children do three or four days a week. They silently read the chapter or two that I have assigned for the day. Then they write in the log for about ten minutes. I tell them to write what they were thinking as they did their silent reading, which, I am aware, is a notion new and strange to many of them. "I'll be helping you out in the first few weeks," I tell them.

I model what I mean by "thinking while reading" in two ways. First, I choose a book at random from our classroom library, read aloud a passage, then turn my head to the side and have a conversation with myself about what I was thinking as I read. Then I read a few excerpts from logs written in the past, though not about the books they're getting ready to choose.

"I'll go through your response log," I say, "and highlight in yellow all the words that show you are thinking as you read. Saying, 'This chapter was good, I liked it,' is not thinking," I tell them, "unless you tell why."

When I go through the logs, I highlight Kathleen's strong response to *Sounder:* "I suddenly felt sad, mad, and like I'm going to throw up all at the same time when I read the part about the bull and the horse doctor." Robin, who is not a very good reader, gets a highlight for "I was thinking in this book who were the slaves in Georgia," but no highlight for "In Ch 2, this is what I thought about. One night in the little boy's house and the father was taken away." Retelling events is not the same as thinking.

Tammy, who has learning disabilities, gets a highlight for "My favorite part so far is when they describe Greta and Ky's window boxes." Until this year, Tammy has been part of a pull-out reading resource program, but now she's part of the *Snow Queen* group (Andersen 1985). She chose the book, she said, because she liked the pictures.

Once persuaded that a child has the right idea, I stop highlighting. Kara, for example, gets the idea right away:

I hope Sounder is alive. I don't understand how much of his ear was shot off by the way they described it. It sounds like the whole thing. In the picture he has both ears. I wonder if ears can grow back or not. I hope they can.

So I highlight everything in her first response (much longer than the excerpt here) and tell her, by commenting in the log, that she won't need highlighting anymore. After the first few weeks, I no longer need to highlight anybody's log, though I read them with great interest and I may remind some children, in my written comments, that more thinking, more response, is needed.

I stay out of the response log as a teacher responder. They know I read the log, and I'll write a word or two to confirm this. "Good" and "try to say why you think these things" are typical comments. But I don't want the log to become a conversation between the child and me, so I don't ask questions in the margins. The log should remain a notebook of the writer's thoughts addressed to the writer, to be used as a tool for discovery and a reminder of things to say in the book group meeting.

When I stay out of the response log as a conversational partner, the children tune in more and more to the voice in the head. The voice begins to speak, and they begin to listen. For some children this has been going on for years; they take themselves seriously enough that they listen to themselves. But for others, the inner voice is fragmentary, or it's only a voice of authority coming in from the outside. These children haven't given their own inner voices a chance to develop.

With a spiral notebook open in front of them day after day for ten minutes, they're giving inner voices a chance. The just-completed reading is stimulating to the inner voice: What's going on here? What's happening? Who are these people? The pencil moves, and the brain goes into action. This whole complicated process, because it repeats itself three or four times a week, picks up steam. I can see the children's thinking shape itself on paper.

Next comes the meeting of the book group, when the children who have been reading the same book get together. This happens after three days or so of reading and writing in the log. The composition of the book groups is almost always heterogeneous, a pattern I discovered when I kept records for several years by color coding the names of the students in the groups according to their standardized reading scores. One book, a poetry anthology, drew a disproportionate number of high scorers, but every other book drew a mix of colors.

About the manner of running the book group meeting I say little beyond telling the children to ask one another their questions. Usually the children acknowledged to be "smart" begin the year with the feeling that they alone possess the right answers. "Everybody in the book group talks and asks their questions," I say. "No one has all the right answers. Everybody has some of them." At this point most of the class leaders feel that a burden has been lifted from their shoulders. They can relax and start saying, "I don't know" and "I don't understand." Then, because they are intelligent and pick up this style of thinking right away, they are leaders in passing it on to the others.

The groups may be hesitant getting started, but I've never had a single group of children who couldn't figure out how to talk to one another. At the first meeting, the children often ask each other, "What did she highlight in yours?" Each one talks, even the shy, scared ones, and the hard-core cases. Sometimes the children read from their logs, but mainly they read them silently and then talk. I find it helpful to draw the class together after the meetings to ask, "How did someone help you? How can you do the group meeting better next time?"

By keeping my ears tuned and by reading their logs, I have a pretty good idea what the children are talking about.

"How much of this book is true?" writes Mason about the book *My Brother Sam is Dead* (Collier and Collier 1985). "Tim must really want Sam to be proud of him. I wonder if Sam is going to come back." For Bruce, who hates reading and who came into the class reading below grade level, the log shows a jumble of voices. Consider his incoherent thoughts on paper about the novel *Dear Mr. Henshaw:*

> I don't really like this book. I guess it's OK. But this book is sad. This chapter is about Christmas because he got a jacket and oh yeah people have been taking things from his lunch.

This whole listening process—listening to the inner voice—is still rather tenuous, especially for children like Bruce, who, to keep that voice alive, needs lots of group support. The book group pulls him into the dialogue. Bruce takes his turn in the circle, saying what he has thought, no matter how shakily. He begins to internalize the conversation, writing more and more coherently in his log as he listens to other children.

Kevin, who loved to read, was one of those other children who, just by being a regular member of the book group, demonstrated ways of thinking. He was self-assured and didn't mind saying he didn't know something. The other children liked him and regarded him as smart, clever, and intelligent. Over the course of the year, he was a member of several different book groups, since every four weeks or so the membership of the groups would change as the children chose new books. Each child in the class, no matter how good or poor a reader, got to listen to Kevin think aloud. The first time around he chose an easy book for a fifth grader, *Ramona Forever*, so it became clear to the others, who knew Kevin was one of the brains of the school, that "easy to read" and "hard to read" were no longer good reasons for choosing a book.

The entries in Kevin's response log show the wide range of his thinking. In his notes, he says how he feels as he reads; he evaluates; he asks questions; he shows puzzlement; he says what he discovered or realized; and he shows how he was surprised at things.

Notice, for example, what he says about his feelings as he read *Ramona Forever*:

> Where he was singing a song was funny. I liked the part where Ramona was itching, and the part where the doctor thought of siblingitis . . .
>
> When I found out it was a girl, I was kind of disappointed, I was looking forward to having a boy in the family.
>
> When I read the part that said the baby was cross-eyed, I was surprised.

Typically, he evaluates the author's work, as when he reads a poem from *Shrieks at Midnight* (Brewton 1969):

If I had to choose one poem out of the chapter, it would probably be "Brother and Sister." I'm used to fighting [with brothers] so I thought that was a good one.

He likes writing that makes him visualize.

When I read "The Cremation of Sam McGee," I could see in my mind a picture of a body being cremated and the other dude walking off in the forest. I guess "It Isn't the Cough" was pretty good, but I couldn't make a picture in my mind.

I could mostly get a picture of those [poems]. I felt I was right there when Grandpa died.

He's tough on writing that doesn't deliver an anticipated mental experience.

The poems didn't fit the title of the book. It says, "eerie" and I don't think they are.

He often muses about what he thinks, knows, remembers, or realizes; or, on the negative side, what he does not think, know, and so on. Consider, for example, his reactions to the book, *Landslide,* a story of survival by children who are trapped in a ski chalet by an avalanche (Day 1972).

This chapter was great. I got kinda worried when I found out about the postcards. I didn't understand why she would want to do that. This chapter answered my question. The goats do have something to do with surviving—milk. I never even thought of that. And when Laurent went to get hay for the goats, I didn't know if he'd ever get out of the prison. When I read the part where they got the sandwiches, and he ate two, I didn't think that was a good idea because they should have saved some more.

Kevin teaches the other children not only about good writing but also about good reading as it's done by a ten-year-old. Good readers, for example, say they do not understand. They tell their questions. At the beginning of the year, most of the children are still under the impression that if they say anything, it has to be right, so they're very tentative when they sit down to their first book group meeting.

But with remarkable speed, they begin to pick up the kinds of things that children like Kevin have to say.

They listen, and Kevin learns to listen too. For example, when he says in his log, "I didn't understand that part where Jason and Gareth first appeared" (a response to Lloyd Alexander's *Time Cat* 1985), then I know that he's going to take this question to the book group meeting and that someone else, who never thought he could be as smart as Kevin, gets to tell Kevin something.

The next routine is the writing of the book review, which occurs at the same time for each group, since most of the books written for children of this age are about the same length. After the children have finished the last chapter, I have them use the reading period to write the review. Each child writes a separate review. The review tells the other members of the class (who haven't read the book unless they've done so outside of school) enough about the book to give a sense of it, but it concentrates on the child's reactions to the book and their recommendations to others.

Before the children write their first review, I read to them reviews that have been written by children for the magazine *Stone Soup* and by adults for the newspaper. I tell them why I read reviews: to find out which of the new books I might be interested in reading.

After drafting their reviews, they share them with their book group in the next reading period. At that time, they make a few joint decisions, such as whether or not they should give away the end of the book. One group member might say to another, "I didn't think that was true about the book at all, so I think you should support your view on that," which is something they've learned to do after hearing the discussion of the reviews in September. (The September reviews are pretty paltry, which I'll say more about later.) Then they make a final draft of their review in preparation for presenting it to the class.

The next step, which is crucial, is the discussion on the rug, which I ordinarily hold outside of the reading period and usually in the afternoon. Each book group makes its own presentation, sitting as a panel on folding chairs, while the rest of us, including me, sit on the rug. This is a performance, since one group is in the spotlight, and it's also a class discussion, since questions and comments follow the panel's presentation. I keep a low profile as teacher, but I do participate as a questioning member of the audience. Perhaps the main feature of the discussion is the time we give it. We might spend an hour talking about a single book.

The routine formally begins when the five or six panelists individually read their reviews to those of us in the audience. The audience listens.

Then comes question asking. Children in the audience raise their hands, and panelists call on them. In the beginning, questions are tentative, answers brief. For example, during the discussion of *Sounder,* several panelists had said the same thing—"The family was poor, so poor they were starving." Someone from the audience asked, "Why were they poor?" The answer wasn't exactly satisfactory: "Well, they didn't have money." Judging from the children's faces, the answer only provoked more questions.

"Weren't they farmers?" someone asked. Surely farmers couldn't go hungry, not if food grew in their fields.

The discussion grew a little more intense. The children stopped raising their hands.

"They had a lotta little kids."

"The mother goes around picking nuts from the ground, they must have been hungry."

"Maybe the crops weren't good."
There were a lot of partial answers at this point, and puzzled-sounding guesses.

"The lady she washed clothes for was nice. She was nice to the boy," one child volunteered, as though to point to a bright spot.

"If she was nice, why were they starving?" No one nice would watch starving people and do nothing.

All this time, during the musing and questioning, I was quiet. Now I raised my hand. "Didn't it say that they were sharecroppers?" I asked.

The panelists nodded.

"Do you know what sharecroppers are?" When I explain that sharecroppers often ended up with only a share of what might have been a poor crop to begin with, some of the children realize that they've heard of such arrangements between owner and tenant before. But the farms known to them are agrobusinesses—the lettuce and artichoke fields of central California—and they can't imagine a farm with so meager a return. It's at points like this that four or five conversations break out around the rug, and I sometimes have to call the children back to listening to one person at a time. They're like adults that way.

They're also like adults in their amazement when they hear how other people live and what it's like to be poor. This is true of everyone in the class, even those who are themselves poor and know it.

At this point in the conversation about *Sounder*, someone began putting two and two together and asking better, more troubling questions: "I thought these people weren't slaves." (The family in *Sounder* were not slaves, though they were poor, black, and lived in the past. The similarities and differences with respect to the time frame, poverty, and being black all needed talking about. It is at points like this that I take a more vocal role than I did earlier in the discussion.)

"When was Martin Luther King?" another child asked. It's ancient history to them—people, events, and concepts all washing together without apparent differences. We talk on and on, as long as anybody has anything to say.

A few years ago, when I varied the routine somewhat and had two groups of panelists discussing *Sounder* at the same discussion on the rug, there was an amazing exchange between the two groups, group A and group B. Someone in group A asked someone in group B, "What did you think when the father got taken to jail? Did you think he deserved it?"

"Well, no," the child responded. The answer of group B, once its members muddled it out, was that he got taken to jail in spite of being innocent. Someone in the novel had said he did nothing wrong.

Several people in group A, looking pleased with themselves, said they had discussed this very point in their book group. Several times, in fact. They realized that the person in the novel who defended the father was wrong: the father had stolen the pig, and the reason they knew this was that the family was eating ham at the very moment the sheriff came to the house.

Someone in group B said its members didn't discuss this point at all. They figured that if someone said the father hadn't done anything wrong, then he couldn't have stolen the pig.

At this, the people in group A looked smug. It was as if they were thinking, "Aha! see what happens when you don't talk things out as you should?" I almost wanted to laugh, but I remained quiet. I didn't say a thing. I was pleased that some of the children had paused to question a character's credibility. I liked their persistence in returning to the question several times. Even more, I was pleased at the length of time the class was able to stay interested in the question, tossing it back and forth.

Even when the children all were convinced that the father had actually stolen the pig, they seemed uncomfortable with the conclusion that he was a wrongdoer. Here they returned to the question I mentioned earlier: "Why were they so poor?" They were still seeking explanations to the question of who or what was to blame for stealing the pig. This is the sort of thing that no teacher teaches or even expects; but when it happens, you think, "Well, maybe I set up the environment where this could happen, and that's good."

In discussions on the rug I try to cultivate an atmosphere of group talk in which we're all wonderers and puzzlers. Once in a while I'll simply be an information giver; I'll say what a sharecropper is. But for the most part, I'm there as a model question asker. As an audience member, I can also keep the children from quitting their discussion too soon. I make sure that they have all the time they need to return to interesting or bothersome questions.

The last step, putting the book out for others to borrow, also is important: in a community of readers, people borrow books. When the discussion is finished, the panelists put their folding chairs away. Then they put their copies of the novel on the metal spinning rack at the back of the classroom. The reviews are added to the loose-leaf binder in our class library. The book now is finished as far as group work goes. No group can pick this book in the future because it's been discussed on the rug already. However, copies of the book now are ready for individuals to sign out and take home. The children have a pretty good idea whether they want to read it because they've listened to the recommendations—lukewarm or enthusiastic—of other children whose reading tastes they're familiar with.

The critical point that I had missed for many years of teaching language arts should now be clear: children pick up language with remarkable speed from other children. Not to use other children as a resource is a shame and a waste. What we've done for years, in the name of helping the inept readers at the bottom of the class, is to remove them from the source of greatest help. Ability grouping keeps those in need of language away from those who use it well. Tracking, as a system, keeps them from hearing the other children's language.

Spoken language is the medium by which children become part of a reading community. It's been my observation over the years that the sooner children learn how to speak "book group talk," the sooner they begin to think while they read. Thinking, I know from watching my children, is hard. The inner voice stops, trails off, or never gets started. In the small group, children support each other. Each can say something, even if only a brief remark, and in time, they all learn how to talk about books. I'm now convinced that "thinking while you read" is internalized book talk, which allows children to feel, visualize, and get perturbed, just as they do when they talk aloud about books.

Kevin and a few others in the class could speak both silently inside their heads and socially in the group. The response logs of these people were stimulating to read—full of wonderful thoughts—from September onward. These are the logs I copied to read to future classes. But the logs of most of the children—Robin and Bruce and others—didn't become interesting until later in the year. The same was true for the book reviews, which the children presented as panelists. In September most of the children had little to say; they merely adopted the formulaic language of the book report. They listed the characters, announced that "this takes place on a farm" (a nod toward "setting"), gave chunks of the plot, and ended with "I liked this book" or "this was a good book." By January, they knew that the people sitting on the rug were not going to be interested unless they said something more. They had played their speaking roles so often, both in numerous book group meetings and discussions on the rug, that when they sat down to write, the voice of the muse was right there. By spring, I had little doubt that in most cases, the voice talked to the children while they wrote their reviews.

The secret, if there is one, is to keep the children's attention on themselves as question askers and to simultaneously move them back and forth between talking aloud and talking silently. This encourages the internalization of book group language. The sequence of activities in the book cycle does this in both short- and long-term ways. In the short term, the sequence moves the children from the book group (talking aloud), to reading and writing in the log (talking silently). In the long term, over the course of the four-week book cycle, the sequence moves them through a series of discussions on the rug, each eliciting more elaborate question asking than the one before. Having finished one cycle, they practice again during the course of the next.

My last point is a reminder about social role. In the rush to teach children "better" thinking, I must remind myself continually that I have told the children their role is to ask their own questions. I have to remember that the questions are really theirs and that they don't always ask the questions I would ask. If Sounder is injured, they want to know how bad. Or they want to know how big something is. "How big are badgers?" one child asked during a discussion of *Incident at Hawk's Hill* (Eckert 1972). In addition, unlike me, they're fascinated with the relationship between books and movies, and books and television. "Would it be hard to train a badger to act in a movie?" one child wanted to know when the others got to talking about turning books into movies.

In the end, thinking comes about because the child has acted out an appropriate social role, which the class as a whole has learned how to play. The children have shown one another how to do it. Who has taught the class? "We're all teachers here," I say, "and I'm the tallest."

NINE

Who Should Evaluate Reading and How?

Suzie How well does your child read? How good is the teacher's reading program?

Perhaps no educational questions occupy the American public more than these. As anxiously as traders watch the rise and fall of the Dow-Jones averages, the American public watches the test scores for reading: two points up, three points down. A *New Yorker* cartoon, poking fun at popular attitudes, shows a wild-eyed crowd running pell-mell down a New York street, while behind the crowd stands a beast looking like a cross between a dinosaur and King Kong, his mouth open in a roar, his long-clawed front feet grasping two spindly skyscrapers. Yells one frenzied member of the crowd to another: "Just when citywide reading scores were edging up!"

Teachers like Suzanne, who come from a social philosophy of teaching, have a problem finding a fit between popular attitudes of this kind and reading instruction.

No one has yet suggested that standardized tests should be discarded, ingrained as they are in the American way of gaining admission to college and grad school. But many people, including the cartoonist, suggest that Americans have become hysterically single-minded when it comes to curves, stanines, and percentiles—in short, "accountability."

One critic, summing up the findings of a commission on standardized testing, cites five reasons why it's wrong for evaluators to look only at standardized tests (O'Neal 1991).

1. The tests themselves are imperfect, showing only what children do in a brief period of time on a paper-and-pencil task and not what children do when they really read.

2. The tests are unfair to minority groups. The discrepancy between Anglo and minority children is greater on standardized tests than in school performance.

3. The tests take up too much instructional time. Some children spend weeks taking standardized tests. One complaining first-grade teacher began to name the ones she was required to give: tests for gifted and talented, for the Chapter One reading program, for progress in reading readiness, for progress in basic skills, not to mention tests for vision and hearing, for scoliosis, and for aptitude in art and music. There were more to give, she said, but she refused to give them.

4. The tests dictate teaching methods, even to the point where teachers teach reading and writing by having students practice the format of the test.

5. Misinformation abounds. People easily draw wrong conclusions from the typically brief reports of test scores published in local newspapers. SAT scores, for example, are reported in some local papers as statewide averages

compared with the averages in other states. What's left out of the reports is the fact that some state universities do not require the SAT for admission; they require the ACT instead. As a result, the so-called ACT states have only a small number of SAT takers—these being the students applying to out-of-state, usually Ivy League colleges—and therefore, the SAT averages in these ACT states are sky-high. Comparing averages is a foolish game that does little except distract the public's attention from real problems.

Betsy, from my HART group, puts testing in perspective. "A paper and pencil test is a piece of the picture, just a piece" (Brandt 1991). Would passing the written test for driving, she asks, convince anyone that their son or daughter is ready to take the car and go driving? Wouldn't that parent and wouldn't the bureau of motor vehicles want to know more? Reading, she insists, is the same. The test score tells us something, but it's not enough.

The new word in reading evaluation—now competing with *accountability*—is *authentic*, meaning that what evaluators should look at are the real things children do in the ordinary course of reading either at home or in school. In many schools, teachers have borrowed from the teaching of writing the idea of the portfolio. Why not, they say, have a portfolio for each child, in which both the teacher and the child place materials showing progress in reading? In each folder, each year, they would place a list of books read. The child puts in samples from the response log. Both the teacher and the child contribute a narrative saying what sorts of things the child read and whether, and in what way, the child was engaged. By adding to the same portfolio year after year, the school indicates its interest in development over the long range. Researchers wanting evidence of children's reading can examine whole portfolios.

"Authentic" evaluation is based on everyday values. If a teacher asked his or her sister-in-law how her child was reading, she might say, "He loves to read, he's always reading. He just likes certain kinds of books, though—adventure stories, never any information books." Or she might say, "I'm a little worried. He does all right on his standardized tests, but just all right. I have to push him to sit down with a book. He doesn't enjoy it, and when he's finished, he can't say what he read." Consider what the sister-in-law values: whether or not her child is reading, what he reads, how well he scores on the tests, but especially how eagerly or reluctantly he sits down to read. Notice that she connects his enjoyment of reading with whether or not he can say something about it when he finishes. As an evaluator, the sister-in-law is interested in the standardized test score but only as a piece of the more interesting picture of her child's growing engagement with books, magazines, and newspapers.

Suzanne's taping project for the writing groups was authentic evaluation; it was her way of watching children in the act of learning to see how they were coming along. She captured the quality of their engagement by assessing the thinking quality of their language.

Now the two of us turned to reading. "How," I asked her, "do you evaluate reading?"

Suzanne Ah, yes. How do I know the children are making progress? Teachers I've talked to about teaching reading as "thinking while you read" are at first skeptical, even suspicious. There's a conspicuous lack of testing. To these teachers, it all seems too easy. I think they wonder how they can evaluate without workbooks and tests, without prepared questions with right and wrong answers. Even parents who tell me they have noticed an increased interest in reading at home may be nervous at first. Not all parents are happy just because their child is thinking while he or she reads.

I remember one parent who was really irate when she realized what we were doing. She came storming in unannounced after school one day, and told me in no uncertain terms that her child had tested poorly in the state they'd just moved from, and that she'd been assured I was a good teacher when he was enrolled in Monte Vista. Yet here the children were, just sitting around reading with no workbooks and no skills tests, and I wasn't teaching the reading groups. Her voice got louder, her face redder. She wasn't going to stand for it, and was going to report me to the school board!

Well, I said, as calmly as I could, if she wanted Timmy placed in another class I'd certainly understand, but we would miss the contributions he was making to his book group. His growth in thinking was certainly evident in his response log, I said, which I whipped out from his desk and placed within her reach.

For Timmy's mother and skeptical others, the persuasive evidence is right there in the logs, where the children's voices appear on the page. At parent conferences, I share the logs with parents, who are generally surprised at the range of their children's thinking. Honesty compels me to say that I never got Timmy's mother to see what I was showing her; neither did she say anything when his impressive test scores came back in the spring. But almost all other parents see in the response log a reflection of their child as a puzzler, an asker, or an appreciator of good plot and funny lines.

The response log isn't a test, but it's a much better way than a test to check the children's comprehension. The logs keep me in touch and tell me what I need to know. They show me vividly what the children are thinking—or in some cases, *not* thinking—and also *how* they think. I read each group's logs once a week, which for me is just a few logs every day. As the year passes, I watch the logs for signs that wondering, puzzling, and questioning are going on.

Consider, for example, the case of Regina, who before the fifth grade had always been in the low reading group, had gone to the resource teacher for extra help, and was now being told to seek that help from other children in her group. One thing that Regina didn't know was that mansions on large estates, especially those in England, were likely to have libraries. She kept wondering in her response log why the girl in the mystery kept going off to the library, which she envisioned to be many miles away in town. I was reading her log periodically, but I kept quiet and wrote a little note, "Why not bring this up in book group?" I just wanted to see if she would pose the question. Then, in one of the book group discussions, she must have brought it up. She wrote in her next response, "The library was right there in the house!"

Suzie Many teachers think of writing in the margins as paper grading. To them, that's evaluation. What you said to Regina in the margin, is that evaluation?

Suzanne
········

It was a suggestion, not really an evaluation. I don't give grades on the logs. I give a reading grade on the report card, but that's my overall evaluation of how well the children are thinking. It encompasses their thinking throughout the whole cycle—from choosing the book to putting it back on the spinner. But fairly often I give little directives like the one I gave Regina. I'm watching and listening all year, giving little nudges when I think they might be doing better. I put a question mark in the margin next to some muddled thinking or handwriting I can't decipher. Or I put an exclamation point in the margin next to a reevaluation or discovery. I encourage longer response by drawing an arrow pointing down the page next to "More! More! Good thinking!" Or I'll write a reminder, "You have as much time as you need to read and think, but ten minutes of writing should be longer than this." Each time I read a log, I write the date after the last entry so that the next time I pick it up I'll know where to begin reading. And most of the time, that is all I do.

I don't give grades. And I don't respond to the children's questions when I write in the logs. Too much intervention shifts the focus from the reader's inner conversation to what I, the teacher, want. I'm doing more of what I did when I highlighted their first journals with yellow: helping them figure out how to be better responders to the people in their group. The logs simply keep me in touch. I feel that I'm listening in on their thoughts as they talk to themselves about the book; I'm an eavesdropper.

I eavesdrop in other situations as well, when I think this will help me understand the level of the children's thinking. For example, when the book groups are meeting, I might have a sudden need for a book from the back shelf or an item from the paper drawer. I set out across the room, wending my way through kids, chairs, and desks, which are clumped together into groups. There is no straight path from front to back. As I step over backpacks, I obviously have to slow down. My ear picks up fragments of book talk.

"Well," I hear Lani say insistently, "I want to know why Jonathan (in *The Fighting Ground* (Avi 1987), a story about the Revolutionary War) thinks it's so great to go off and fight when he's just a kid!" Lani is our class worrier.

"I said," says Joe, "that he probably thinks like . . . it's gonna be fun . . . like exciting . . . like he could be a hero."

Marty agrees. "Yeah, he's not thinking he might get hurt or even killed because this is new stuff for him."

"But his father already is wounded and won't even talk about it," warns Lani.

"Yeah, but like that's somebody else and not him."

"But war is dangerous! Huh, Mrs. Brady!"

I solemnly nod my agreement. War is indeed dangerous. The children know I'm there, and they might even summon me to the group for moral support on occasion, but mainly I'm an outsider to the circle.

That is exactly what I want to have happen. Any intervention from me should be casual, rather than seen by the children as planned. If I see some problem that is not being resolved in logs or groups, I will bring it up during the discussion on the rug, but right now I'm just eavesdropping.

I also evaluate by looking at the book reviews, not only for growth in the children's abilities to comprehend but also for growth in the mechanics of writing. This is the only type of writing that is consistently coming in, in final draft, ready to be published as a class book, that I do not see until it is finished. On all the other writing projects, I help the children edit. Looking at these reviews, I can keep track of progress in handwriting, spelling, paragraphing, and other mechanical skills. I can address these in minilessons or in later editing conferences during writing workshop time.

And then what? At year's end, I ask the children to take all of the books they've read in groups during the year and put them in a pile with the best on top, followed by the next best, and so on. The books they've read but don't have copies of they represent with pieces of cardboard. They make momentous decisions as they arrange and rearrange the piles. They're very interested in, even surprised at, others' choices. One child's favorite is number six on another child's desk. The children talk about their opinions and standards for selection. All of this is evaluation.

"I loved this book, it's my all-time favorite" mostly satisfies as the qualification for number one, and few children really dislike number six.

Choices in the middle have a more literary tone:

"This was a fantasy and I like realistic better."

"The main character was too nerdy for me."

"This one kept up the suspense."

"I like all Madeleine L'Engle's books."

"This one was too long" (or "too short").

"I didn't like the ending."

"This one didn't keep my interest."

"I liked it halfway through and then I didn't and then I did."

"The first eleven chapters were all boring but the last chapter was exciting."

Near the end of each semester, I also ask the children to write me evaluation letters, telling me anything they want to say about themselves and reading. "I used to . . . but now" is a favorite theme. "I used to hate to read but now it's fun." Or "I never used to read but now I read at home and at school." One year, when the reading-whole-books program was new and I wanted to hear their reactions, I had them write to me in late November. Regina, like most of the others, saw a difference between "a book," meaning a whole book, and "the reading book," meaning a basal reader with selections from books and textbook questions at the end of each selection:

Nov. 20

I like reading in a book. I do not like reading in the reading book because it is boring. All you do is read the story and answer the quishons. What I realy like about reading in a story book is that you can talk about it with other people and you can meet other people and you can shair your thoughts. And you can learn about working together.

by
Regina

The evaluation letters the children write at the end of the year (see Figure 9–1) include suggestions for books I should read aloud, books they recommend for next year's book selections, and books I should retire to the cupboard. Sometimes the children suggest report-card grades for themselves or tell me what they plan to read during the summer. They mention specific book groups or book reviews, which they characterize as troublesome or "awesome."

I evaluate.

They evaluate.

The parents also evaluate in a sense, because I listen with great care to what they tell me in parent conferences about their children's reading at home. This is the reading of books the children borrow from the metal spinner. This reading is important to the building of a lifelong reading habit—keeping a book nearby and reading every day—so I hang on every word these parents tell me.

"I used to get him a book at the library. Now he wants to get his own book."

"She likes to talk about her books now. She tells me what *I* ought to read!"

The last piece of the evaluation picture goes into place in May, when the children take the standardized California Test of Basic Skills (CTBS).

They score wonderfully well. Those who initially were below average show the most dramatic growth. They were the ones who complained the first day we did response logs, "I don't know what to write because I don't think when I read." Timmy, whose mother came to scold me at the beginning of the year, scored 10.3 (90th percentile) at the end, an improvement of 5.6 years over the previous year. Regina scored 5.7, an improvement of 1.3 years.

The class average on the whole battery—all the math and English tests together—is two to three years above grade level, but the lump score doesn't tell me as much as the breakdown. The reading comprehension score is consistently out in front of such others as the vocabulary score. It might be three or more years above grade level, compared with two years and a bit above grade level for vocabulary.

Dear Mrs Brady,

Last year I never read because I didn't have to. My teacher didnt ashighne us to. I really haded reading and didn't care! This year I began to read at home and school and found out how much fun it can be.

I think I get a B or S be cause I am not a super wr reader. I hope I can be able to read some storys as good as Save queen of Sheba and charlie the lost Dog.

I'an really a bookworn. I get into a good book and their is no stopping me. I clike books that are exciting and hard to put down.

FIGURE 9-1   Children's Evaluation of Their Reading (Unedited)

There's a reason for this difference. Comprehension is a test of "thinking while you read," and I think that the children are now relaxed enough about reading that, for the first time ever, all of them finish the test. No longer do they read a passage, read the questions, then read the passage to find answers. Instead, they read, answer questions, and go on. They have thoughts, which they hold onto as they read the questions. They feel confident and in control. This is entirely different from the approach many of them took earlier, which was to hunt through the words, looking for the ones that were the "right answers." I know that some children used to read the questions first, before ever reading the passage, and then went back to the passage and scoured it. No wonder they didn't finish the test.

The gap between the two kinds of scores—the comprehension and the vocabulary—shows up most dramatically for children at the low end. One child, I remember, came into the class with scores several years below grade level and a reputed IQ of 80—whatever this might mean. He ended up a year above grade level on comprehension—almost seventh-grade level—but he still showed the equivalent of a second-grade level on vocabulary. Now what did I make of this? I think he had learned to make sense while he read, but he still hadn't learned to do what schools and test makers wanted him to do, which was to define words out of context. But defining words out of context was far less important for this youngster's survival than comprehension. The comprehension score is the more important score. It tells me how confident children are in thinking while they read, in making the words make sense.

I've put my thoughts on evaluating reading into table form (see Figure 9–2). If you look at the reading evaluation table, you'll see that the value on thinking while reading, which Suzie and I call the "quality of engagement," is prominent in column one. This is the *what* of evaluation, what is being evaluated. Column two shows the *how*, the method of seeking evidence. Column three shows the *who* of evaluation, who evaluates: the teacher, the children, the parents, and the school district's evaluation office.

What's important is the way these three—the what, the how, and the who—work together. Column four shows the character, or style, of this evaluation.

READING EVALUATION

What's evaluated?	What's collected or observed?	Who evaluates? (is there a grade?)	Style of evaluation?
quality of engagement (thinking while you read)	response log collected	the teacher, no grade	authentic
=	Book Group meeting observed	the teacher, no grade	authentic
= (and mechanics of writing)	Book Reviews collected	the teacher, no grade	authentic
quality of engagement (thinking while you read)	Panel/Discussion on the rug observed	the teacher, no grade	authentic
=	Report of reading at home (Homework Schedule, see ch. 11)	the teacher, no grade	authentic

The teacher gives a grade on all of the above at report card time.

What's evaluated?	What's collected or observed?	Who evaluates? (is there a grade?)	Style of evaluation?
=	Piling books in order of preference (and commenting on reading experience)	the children	authentic
=	Write a letter evaluating self as reader	the children	authentic
=	Commenting in conference with teacher	the parents	authentic
comprehension, vocabulary	CTBS (Cal Test of Basic Skills)	the district Office of Evaluation	standardized test

FIGURE 9–2

Suzie   Suzanne either has it lucky in her school district or else she has met the testing dragon and slain him already. Mention standardized tests, and she shows no fear. Ask her whether her district's evaluation office invades her classroom with standardized tests, and she says, "No, the testing happens only once a year; we're really not invaded." Inquire whether standardized tests dictate her curriculum, and she responds, "No, and in fact, it's probably the test scores that made it possible for me to change my reading program away from the basal program. The high scores gave me freedom. It would be hard for the administrators to argue against the program because they'd be arguing against their own definition of success. At the same time, I'd be very pleased to do away with standardized tests altogether."

Suzanne gives the tests. She interprets the results. She's in control. At the same time, she's aware that not every teacher is as willing or able as she is to examine the test results critically and say, "Certain parts of this test, namely the comprehension, are more important than others." Not only are other teachers uncritical of tests, but many of them look to the test to tell them precisely what to teach and the form in which to teach it. They march in time with the test so closely that it's hard to tell whether the test is designed to fit the curriculum or the curriculum is designed to fit with the available test.

In Hawaii one year, I sat in an auditorium where testing experts conducted a one-hour workshop on the meaning and purpose of the statewide writing test. As we were all leaving the auditorium, a teacher told me with relief, "This is so much better. Last year they didn't tell us which form of the writing test they were going to use—you know, *narrating,* or *describing,* or *explaining,* or *arguing.* I really didn't know which one to teach. I feel better now since I know it will be *explaining.*"

My own writing program at the University of Hawaii has a good placement test for expository writing, but the test is now, in fact, a curriculum guide for writing in many high school English classrooms. What, I wonder, has happened to the writing of poems and stories? Must we have a test for these, too, to argue their value with teachers?

Teaching to the test not only puts blinders on the teacher, it also puts the teacher in a subordinate relationship to the testing office. One of the darkest sides of the testing debate is that children ultimately learn a top-down, authoritarian style. The teacher learns this don't-ask-questions style from the administration, and the children learn it from the teacher.

When authentic evaluation enters the picture, the source of authority changes. Authentic evaluators look to the professional judgment of teachers: they evaluate ongoing work that teachers deem important. Quite suddenly, teachers are thrust into the professional role of interpreting behavior and figuring out what evidence should be collected so that the interpretation can be done. When Suzanne said "no more workbooks and no more workbook tests," she had to devise what to put in place of the tests—the response logs, her observation of book groups, and so forth. Elsewhere, the popular whole language movement has made many others question the usefulness of skills tests. They, too, face the sometimes difficult question of what to put in place of these tests. When it comes to finding alternative means of evaluation, they find themselves feeling uncertain.

Such was the case with KEEP in Honolulu: the Kamehameha Early Education Project for grades K–3. KEEP is funded by the Kamehameha Schools, which is an institution privately endowed for educating the children of Hawaii's indigenous people. The difference between KEEP and Suzanne's case was that the KEEP teachers were led into the program by curriculum specialists rather than initiating it themselves.

Under the old reading system, the KEEP teachers evaluated the children's progress by keeping a scope-and-sequence chart. Down the side of the chart were listed skills (called "reading strands"):

- listening/reading comprehension
- information retrieval
- vocabulary
- phonics/word structure
- sight vocabulary

Across the top were listed "objectives," each strand having so many of these objectives and each objective matched up with a multiple-choice test. Every teacher knew the sequence: when a child passed one test, he or she was ready to begin work on the next. The teachers knew what to teach because each objective was specific about what material to cover. Once tested on consonant sounds, the child was ready for digraphs and blends, and so on.

The chart for the new system—which looked a little like Suzanne's table—was altogether different from the old chart. Now having dispensed with tests, the teachers were to collect reading logs and writing samples, do interviews with the children, and make observations of what the children did while they read.

When members of KEEP's evaluation staff interviewed eight teachers who were using the new system, they found that most of the teachers were uncomfortable with the new procedures (Yumori and Tibbets 1991). They were uncomfortable not because the procedures were difficult but because the picture of what they were accomplishing had suddenly grown cloudy. Said one teacher, "We want to know where students are in [terms of] skills." Said another: "In KROS [the old system] you know exactly what they know—plurals, initial consonants, etc." Said a third: "What skills do I need to work on with specific groups?" Most felt nostalgic for the old system. Their new relationship with evaluation and evaluators was rough going.

Only a few of the teachers took easily to their new roles as authentic evaluators, these being the teachers who trusted their abilities to observe progress in the students' on-going reading and writing. Like Suzanne, they assumed that they could evaluate by watching their students in action or just working with them. Said one: "From normal observation . . . I can tell a lot." The word *normal*, like the word *everyday*, tells the story. According to this view, evaluation is something a teacher does in the normal course of events. These same teachers found it useful to show the student portfolios to parents, figuring that parents, too, would be able to appreciate the children's progress by looking at their everyday work.

I talked to Suzanne about the question "Why should the two groups of teachers view evaluation so differently?" Somehow I didn't believe that the difference lay in capability. All of the teachers, I suspected, were able to evaluate children's ongoing work as well as they could grade tests.

"Grading tests is what we've been brought up on," said Suzanne. "It's not that teachers must have an answer key or they won't know the answers, or even that they don't know when a child shows signs of becoming a better reader. It's their job description that counts. It's been their job for a long time to ask other people's questions and to be objective.

"As in 'fair and objective'?" I asked.

"As in 'fair and objective,'" she said. "A test on digraphs and blends asks every child to give the same answer. In the higher grades, I've seen teachers ask trivial questions—'What was the color of the main character's eyes?'—because the fact of having only one answer makes it objective. Didn't get the answer? Well, too bad. At least the teacher was fair. That sort of thing. Most teachers are not simple-minded—at least they don't begin their careers that way. But testing encourages teachers to trivialize."

"Why can't there be better tests?" I asked.

"There *are* good tests," she responded, "but they're the kind with more than one right answer, and no answer key or machine scoring. Every time we decide to give these better tests, teachers are put in the spot of authentic evaluators. Decisions are hard to make. The answers are not as clear anymore. The level of discomfort rises, as it did for the teachers you were talking about who wanted to go back to the old scope-and-sequence chart and the tests on 'objectives.'"

"So in the end, you think teachers have to accept whatever discomfort authentic evaluation carries with it?"

"Yes, I do," she told me. "We're talking about teacher professionalism, which I guess I feel quite strongly about. Are teachers going to stick with trivial questions because of the comfort level for the teacher or will they evaluate what's most valuable for children as readers?"

"It's that simple?"

"It's that simple."

Suzanne As schools have turned more and more to standardized testing, they
have separated evaluation from teaching, moving it downtown to a
department of evaluation. Authentic evaluation is a move to bring
teaching and evaluation back together, bringing evaluation back to
the school site. If you go in and ask good teachers, "How is so-and-
so doing?" they can tell you immediately. They don't have to open
their grade books. If a parent drops in to ask, "How has so-and-so
done this week?" you just know. You don't say, "Gosh, I'll look in his
desk and see what he's doing." The very explicit manual, the scope-
and-sequence chart, and the multiple-choice test were ways of
putting evaluation in the hands of someone else and saying, "You
judge." I can see why authentic evaluation makes teachers uncomfortable. All of a sudden, they're having to say, "*I* judge."

I realized, as I talked to Suzie, that I continually do two kinds of
evaluating. One is judging the learning that's going on and the other
is judging curriculum itself. Searching for value in the curriculum is
what I began years ago when I finally decided that I had the ability
to judge. I began then to ask myself: "Is this worthwhile? Is this time
well spent?"

For example, in reading, I still think that children's fiction is a
good vehicle for turning children into lifelong, active learners, but I
would be worried if the children failed to become interested in
nonfiction and newspapers. So I have them read fiction for reading
and nonfiction—books and newspapers—for social studies. Fiction
and nonfiction overlap, as it turns out. Fiction such as Avi's novel,
The Fighting Ground (1987), teaches the children about the American Revolution. Newspaper accounts of life in China help them understand the cultural meaning of a novel such as Bette Bao Lord's *In
the Year of the Boar and Jackie Robinson* (1986).

Then there's the value of literary study, which we talked about in
chapter 7. Are the concepts "plot" and "conflict" worthwhile for ten-
year-olds? Do I now teach the children about the structure of a literary work or do analyses of character? The answer is yes, within
strict limits.

Once a year, using one book, I teach literary concepts. For the
last few years I've chosen Katherine Paterson's *Bridge to Terabithia*

(1987), and I've used materials from a unit plan worked out by teachers. For example, I teach the children how to think about the plot line—the conflict, rising action, a climax as the rising action peaks, then a resolution. The children get together and, depending on what they think the conflict is, express differing views on where the climax comes. So they talk about that in small groups.

I realize that the rising action concept can be a cliché of literary study, but my children need to understand how stories are put together. Their own stories grow boring, and they don't know why. They write the mall story: "I went shopping and I came home." They write the car chase story: "one car chased another until they crashed, the end." They need to know how authors end stories. We talk about how the end of *Bridge to Terabithia* is really the end, how Jesse lets his little sister Maybelle stay in Terabithia, the secret place where once only he and Leslie had played. Now, I ask them, would the author keep on going from here, saying what games he and his little sister played and so on? No, the action has already peaked, and the reader's question about Jesse—Will he be able to recover from Leslie's death?—is really answered already. This is the end. To have a good ending, the writer has to have rising action to come down from, thus the need for rising action. I can hear this language—"climax" and "ending"—when the children talk to one another about their own writing. Stepping back a bit from personal involvement, they can see themselves as responders to what an author has done and can transfer that insight to themselves as writers.

Most of the children enjoy the book when we do it this way, but when we've finished, someone will usually ask, "Are we going to do our next book like this?"

"We could if you want to," I'll say. "What do you think?"

"No, no, no, we want to go back to the other way," several will say. The other way is choice, ownership, finding their own meaning as readers, and sharing this meaning and their reactions with their peers.

They always want to go back.

So, yes, I do literary study for the purposes I have named. I take great care, though, not to let it overshadow the curriculum's primary object, to turn the class into a society of readers.

Should we use literary works to teach morals or principles? Here is another question of value and what's worthwhile. Stories have taught such lessons since the beginning of time. But I share the concern expressed by Natalie Babbitt, the author of the wonderful children's novel, *Tuck Everlasting* (1975). This author comments that "a good story can collapse if it's made to bear too much weight" (Babbitt 1990). Using stories to teach themes or morals such as social responsibility, as her book is being used, she says, creates the risk of "destroying their magic and making reading a chore, a drag, just another lesson."

Then there are the questions about the value of reading versus writing. There was a time when writing had no time of its own in the daily schedule, and we had to slip it in like an extra frill in the curriculum. Even now, years after the writing revolution, I find I sometimes have to argue that writing—just writing, as in stories, autobiography, and poems—is worth the time. One of the traps in the whole language emphasis on the reading/writing connection is that both activities take a lot of time. Therefore, it's easy to think, "I'll put them both in one period; the writing can cover the topics that the children encounter in their reading." It's true that the children do an enormous amount of writing during reading time, and many teachers think that is enough.

What gets lost in combining the two in this way is the development of the writer's personal voice. The response log is valuable, but it does not fulfill the goals of a writing curriculum. The mere practice of placing writing time after reading time is really too seductive. It's so easy just to keep on writing a sort of response log and call this "learning to write." I try to ensure that the children do their own writing, in their own style, by placing the writing hour before the reading hour. You don't teach them to feel like writers if all their topics are chosen by teachers. It's all a question of how much I value this sense that "I am a writer and I myself make decisions about what to write." This value is high on my list.

Suzie The topics of this chapter have ranged from testing to *Tuck Everlasting,* from the heightened anxiety over test scores to the less sensational debate over the writing/reading connection. Ordinarily, testing would belong to a chapter entitled "Evaluation" or "Assessment" (two words we use interchangeably), while the writing/reading connection would be placed in a completely different chapter, probably called "Reflections on Instructional Practice." In Hawaii's Department of Education there are separate administrative offices, one for evaluation and one for instruction. The evaluation office, as an agency that ostensibly limits itself to looking at output rather than involving itself in planning or goal setting, keeps its distance. Authentic assessment has the effect of integration. So closely is authentic assessment tied to classroom activity—to reflection on the work just completed, to program—that it becomes a part of the overall teaching effort.

Suzanne   It seems natural to join the two kinds of assessment together—evaluating children's work and evaluating curriculum. I do both in the course of a day. I see both as part of my job.

Suzie   Your job rather than the job of administrators in a downtown office.

Suzanne   I've always just assumed that evaluation was my job. In recent years I have guarded my role as evaluator. I've stood over it and defended it when I thought it might be threatened by administrative authorities.

Suzie   And now with the trend toward authentic assessment, what will happen?

Suzanne   Authentic assessment is a recognition that decisions about the means of evaluation cannot be made at some point distant from the classroom. If portfolios are going to be used, or the student's log, or the student's reflective self-evaluation, then evaluating those things is something that teachers must plan to do in the course of instruction.

Suzie Doesn't all this authentic assessment sound like extra work for the teacher?

Suzanne Not more work, unless teachers decide that more is necessary. *Decide* is a key word; authentic assessment means that teachers have to decide on ways of evaluation that fit, like pieces in a puzzle, with the rest of their instruction. They can't say, "Somebody else does all that deciding, and I have no control."

Suzie Authentic assessment means more teacher participation.

Suzanne It means more teacher participation in deciding the form that assessment should take, which means that teachers will need to converse more with other teachers.

Suzie That sounds to me like more work.

Suzanne More conversation and more time, perhaps. But the teachers I have known are ready and willing to spend that time when they see that they are making joint decisions and affecting the course of their schools.

TEN

Scaffolding a Work Ethic

Suzanne As I said in chapter 1, on the first day of school I tell the children, "We all work." I use the word *work* deliberately. I'm serious about it. I don't believe that schools give too little work, nor do I think people are generally lazy, but children need to develop healthy values about work. In the last several chapters we've talked about children as teachers of other children in writing and reading. Part of what is needed to make a go of these groups is a shared work ethic. I need a place in the curriculum where I can develop the children's consciousness of themselves as workers. Raising this consciousness is the point of this chapter.

Suzie   As a parent, I remember worrying about ways to teach my own children to feel confident and resourceful about jobs around the house. The classroom is another house, with a different kind of job.

I saw in my university classes a student here, a student there, who came into the class with initiative. They were self-starters who intended to dig into the course assignments and take away something that they had been looking for.

University study is nose-to-the-grindstone work, but the work ethic Suzanne and I describe in this chapter goes well beyond perseverance. It includes as a key element the worker's own thoughtful self-assessment and decision making.

I was introduced to Suzanne's curriculum for teaching a work ethic without being aware of it. She called it her "contract" hour, a time for working on "contracts." I remember arriving in the middle of it on one of the rare occasions when I was able to visit her classroom. I sat down, as Suzanne indicated, at a table with Betsy and Santo (Santo had come from Indonesia for the year). I was puzzled. Everyone in the class seemed intent and serious, yet I couldn't figure out what directions they were following. Betsy was helping Santo with a reading game, drawing him a diagram and explaining it. One child was drawing a picture for another child's published story (I asked them about this). Two were playing Diane Bigham's computer game, "Where in the World is Carmen San Diego?" Two were playing chess while another one watched, a couple were looking at dictionaries, one was searching through *The Guinness Book of World Records,* and several others were doing paper-and-pencil puzzles.

Meanwhile, Suzanne was at her desk deep in conversation with a curly headed girl who bobbed up and down, talking and pointing. "What was she doing?" I asked Suzanne later.

Suzanne   That was contract time, which goes from eleven to noon every day. The children were working on their contracts (see Figures 10–1 and 10–2), and I was making out a new one for Julie, who was negotiating. She wanted to know how many squares were left on her contract, and I said, "Two." She wanted to work on the computer, help in the library, and also take the book she was working on down to the publishing center. That made three things. "Those are three good ideas," I said, so I took away a word puzzle that I had put in one of her squares, leaving room for all three of her choices. That's when she was dancing around the desk.

Suzie   So in each square there's a job to do?

Suzanne   Right, twelve in all. They choose some and I choose some. My choices often come from materials used with gifted children, the one-page word puzzles and math games that I find in *Dynamath, Instructor,* and sources of this kind. As long as I give them things that, with help, I know they can do, I can think of them all as gifted. I call it a contract because the two of us sit together and fill out an individualized agreement.

Suzie   What was Julie allowed to choose?

Suzanne   Almost anything, as long as it would help her learn. She's been watching all the others. She knew there were lots of possibilities. She could choose computer—but just for one of the twelve squares—or do water colors, or do a treasure hunt, which is explained on a wall poster.

Julie's an interesting case. She's earning a good report-card grade for her contract work because she's turned diligent; she is marching through these contracts at a good rate. In earlier school years, she had a poor record, especially in spelling but also in math. The funny thing was, she began to work these math puzzlers, which were something I chose and put on her contract, not anything she would have chosen herself. At first I gave her only easy ones, but she worked her way up. Now she can do the problems in the magazine *Dynamath,* which are not easy.

When I begin the year, most of the children are passive about filling out the contract. I'll say, "What do you want to put in your squares?" and they'll say, "You decide." Then I say, "No, you decide. Would you like computer time or Scrabble?"

Suzie   I thought of college catalogs, with all the options laid out like a contract. Typically, some of the boxes were filled in with institutional requirements, but many of them were left open for student choice.

"What are you going to major in?"

"I'm not sure. My major right now is 'undecided.' That's how they've got me listed in the computer."

Choice was difficult. When I sent my freshmen to the library to select an autobiography from the shelf, they had trouble answering the question "Which of these am I interested in?" But most of them liked the process of making the choice. They felt they were stretching their minds.

Suzanne   Stretching their minds is a point the children grow more conscious of as time passes. At the beginning of the year, as we do the brain unit and study the brain's complexity, potential, and power, the children begin to connect the points of that unit to the contracts, which include all this brain work: the Mindwinders (*Instructor*), the Mind Benders (*Warm-Up Mind Benders*), and other brain teasers and logical thinking exercises. All of these have directions that must be read and followed. These are exercises for their brains, I tell the children, just as the physical education teacher has exercises for their muscles.

As time passes and the children talk about themselves as people with potential, they begin to think of possibilities for the contract.

"Could I make up a word search of explorers?"

"That's an idea."

"Could me and Andrea help Mrs. Vreeland's second graders?"

"All right."

"Could I work on my Boy Scout badge?"

"What do you have to do for the badge?"

"I have to interview my teacher and the principal."

"Sure."

Suzie   I could always spot those students who saw themselves as people having choice. They had such energy. Suzanne told me the story of one of her students who must have been listening to adult conversations about self-esteem and at the same time ruminating on her sense of power. She wrote in her journal, "I have a good shelf of steam." What an image. The child's own store of power was ready to be taken off the shelf and used at an instant's notice.

Robert   Dated __11/15__ to __11/23__

Where in the World? ΔNB 11/18	Graphiti m.a. 11/22
Be Resourceful MY 11/19	Green Dictionary Page 7, Exercise 1 LSR 11/16
Decimal Roller Coaster m.a. 11/22	Natural Features of the U.S. ΔNB 11/18
Picture This! m.a. 11/22 ΔNB 11/18	Math 11/11
September 1990 K.U. 11/23	Mindwinder LSR 11/16
Be a Library Aide Good job! AD 11/15	Computer MY 11/19

FIGURE 10–1   Robert's Contract Cover Sheet

To make Robert's contract, I wrote activities in the boxes as we negotiated, then stapled the cover sheet to eight duplicated puzzles and problems (stacked near my desk). Robert found resources for the other four tasks elsewhere. *ABrady*

"Where in the World"	a map puzzle, *Weekly Reader* Teaching Master
"Graphiti"	a graphing exercise, locating points on a graph, *Graphiti First Quadrant*
"Be Resourceful"	25 questions that require reference material ("What is the circumference of the earth in miles?"), from *Educational Oasis*
Green Dictionary	an exercise on homonyms in one of the classroom dictionaries
"Decimal Roller Coaster"	a math puzzle, connecting decimals with TV shows, then sequencing the decimals (1.21 is less than 12.1), from *Dynamath*
"Nat Features of U.S."	a geography exercise, locating mountains, rivers, on a U.S. map (a *Weekly Reader* Teaching Master)
"Picture This!"	a math crossword puzzle, *Dynamath*
Math 11/11	a revision of your math homework for November 11
"September 1990"	a prefix puzzle, one item for each of the days of September, *Weekly Reader* Teaching Master
"Mindwinder"	goofy game with words and line drawings, *Instructor*
Be a Library Aide	a chance to help the school librarian for half an hour
Computer	a chance to use the classroom computer for half an hour

FIGURE 10–2 Guide to Robert's Contract

I remember those students who were practiced in the art of making choices. They were finished with the dread of decision making. They charged ahead, as if fueled by the process. One student, I recall, bought himself a blue binder when it came time to look for his first job after college. In the binder he carried on a conversation with himself that he had practiced many times earlier. "What to do now?" he wrote. "Maybe I could . . . and maybe I could . . ." The "maybes" became option A and option B, and so forth. There was a different page for each option. Down the center of each page the student drew a line and wrote pros on one side, cons on the other. Then he came to my office where we talked and he decided there were still more options. He added more pages, more pros and cons. He decided he had questions, so he went to the career counselor on campus. He began a new page for things he felt he had better do. He did some of these, thought of more as he went, and added these things to the list. He liked checking off the ones he had finished, then, even when the rejections came, he told me, he accepted them as part of the process. There was plenty more on the list to do.

I felt admiration not only for the student but for the set of teachers who in this student's life had first shown him how to think this way.

Suzanne   I began using contracts long before I recognized them as a tool for
....   teaching children to show initiative and be imaginative in their work. Back in the seventies, when I began using them for first graders, I simply wanted to give the children who finished their other work early something to do.

So I did something simple. I drew five or six large circles in a random pattern on a piece of paper headed with the child's name and the date. In the circles I wrote words or other symbols—for example, the word *paint,* the symbols R-3 for reading game number three, and M-6 for a box of math cubes. I chose the same activities for everybody. Each child knew there were other things they wanted to do: tutor Yoshi on color words, draw a picture, or read a book with Laura. So I wrote the child's choices into some of the circles, then, mindful of that particular child's abilities, I chose one more activity, perhaps a reading game if the child could already read.

Then I began to notice how seriously the children took this work. Contracts were the most exciting part of the day. If their contract included "paint," they watched to see when one of the classroom easels was free and then went up to paint their picture. Meanwhile, they worked on the other jobs, following directions, finding things in the classroom. Some of the items were worksheets, dittoed and attached to the contract. The children had to decide, based on their desires and the availability of the materials, in what order to do the tasks. They had to get the teacher or an aide to sign in the circle when tasks were finished. This was their work. They liked being in charge and having choices. This was real school.

These babies thought they could do anything. They pushed the boundaries. Realize that in those days we were going "back to basics." Curriculum, teaching methods—even the number of minutes to be spent on each subject—were predetermined and controlled by people far away from the classroom. Everyone marched in lockstep, both children and teachers. But these children were going beyond the normal routine, getting out of the "basics" line, showing me how they could learn better and faster in ways that I had not yet seen. I'll never forget the day a youngster brought a board game, Chutes and Ladders, for sharing time, then asked me if he could play the game as part of his contract. "It teaches me to count," he said.

"Oh," I thought, "that's true." I began to realize that when these children saw themselves as scholars, they chose to do things that would help them learn.

Suzie   So when you transport the contract into fifth grade, and you change the six circles into twelve rectangles, I suppose what you keep is the element of contractual arrangement. Some spots are filled with the teacher's requirements, some with the child's choices.

Suzanne   And some are filled with items that I know are not covered in other hours of the school day. I've made promises to the children, that when they arrive at middle school, in the sixth grade, they'll know everything that beginning sixth graders are supposed to know. So that includes, for example, prefixes, and suffixes, and dictionary exercises, which I don't do in my reading program anymore, having dispensed with the reading workbook. Any sort of little thing, that's easy to learn and requires little time when the children put their minds to it, I put on the contract.

Whether offered in the first or the fifth grade, contracts are scaffolds—structured procedures that lead eventually to a sense of personal responsibility. At the beginning, the contract is only a set of procedures: we negotiate the contract one-to-one, the child does each task, makes corrections, gets each one signed by an adult (myself or another adult in the classroom), the child turns it in, I record it, and the child takes it home. But after a while, the children perceive the contract as their "work." I don't exactly take the scaffold down, since the procedural rules stay the same, but the scaffold comes down, you might say, as the children take on responsibility both for getting the contract filled out and finishing the jobs.

As the children's responsibility increases, so does their awareness of the contract's purposes. They say to themselves, "Ah, yes, I see what this contract business is for." They see it as: (1) a place to exercise their brains; (2) a place where the teacher has put everything they need to know for sixth grade; (3) a way to learn how to plan their use of time, which prior to this point they've had little chance to do; and (4) a place where they have input—an opportunity to draw cartoons, for example—and the chance to count it as school work.

A fifth purpose is one that some of the children see right away but others recognize slowly and grudgingly: contracts are for doing what they *need* to do. For some it's accelerated math. For others it's the practice of handwriting, spelling, and multiplication tables—those remedial sorts of things that they did not like doing the first time around and that they never became good at because they rarely put their minds to the task. These children hide what they don't know or can't do, hoping no one will find out. By this time, hiding and hoping has become a painful part of their school day.

Uncovering problems is something we talk about in the brain unit. I tell the children, "Mistakes are good things because they show what you don't know yet." I really have to keep at it, how people who have problems always want to hide them, so I say it repeatedly: "Mistakes are good." Then the day finally comes when I'm making out a contract, and I'll say, "You've got an empty box." The child will sigh, pause, and finally say, "I need to work on my spelling words." For some children, there's a real barrier here that is extremely hard to break through because they've felt bad about this problem—whatever it is—for so long.

Suzie Consciousness is created. It doesn't just happen. The contract creates a time and place for teacher and learner to carry on a consciousness-raising dialogue about work, the first question of which is "What work shall we do?" That question would not arise for the child without the opportunity to fill in the empty squares. A learner doesn't ask, "What work shall I do? what book shall I read? what shall I write about?" unless choice has been offered.

Suzanne and I were part of the generation of young teachers who, in the 1960s, read *Summerhill* (1960), A. S. Neill's engaging book about his boarding school for wayward youth. Unfortunately, that book came to represent choice gone awry, choice without structure or limits. Poorly planned alternative schools set up in those years were said to be following the free-choice policy of Summerhill.

"This is not Summerhill," Suzanne would say. "Children are not playing at being tadpoles. They're not birdies in the trees watching the clouds float by. And this is not free choice."

Free choice presupposes no obligations, the teacher implying by her words that the free-choice activity doesn't need to lead anywhere down the line, only to amuse or occupy the child for the time being. "Making a choice" or "making a decision" is different because it brings in the element of thought about the future. When people "decide" to do something, it means that they have thought about what will happen. They realize they have committed themselves to do what they said they would do. University students understand well the connection between choice and personal responsibility.

Suzanne By and large, my children accept the idea of choice, and, though some do so only after a struggle, they accept the responsibilities that go with the contracts: correcting what they've missed and resubmitting the corrected version. Both are necessary steps to take the contract to completion.

The first contract is one that the children all leap into. Their older brothers and sisters have done contracts in this class, so they've heard something about it. And this first one is easy and fun to do. "I'd never put anything on your contract I don't think you can do," I promise, echoing what I told the first graders years ago. The children are reassured.

In a class of thirty, six or seven children continue to leap from one contract to the next through the year, taking great satisfaction in the whole process. Self-starters, their "shelf of steam" propels them ahead.

Most of the other children need a while to learn how to manage their contract time. Then they settle into a comfortable routine—not driven, not lagging, but chugging along. You can hear them talking, sounding terribly pleased with themselves. "I'm on contract seventeen!" Their admiration for the "super movers"—the children who race through their contracts—is unabashed: "How do you do them so fast?" They see themselves as worthwhile but still needing to change. They have bought into the idea that mistakes are to be noticed, identified, and learned from. They think, "I'm learning, I'm growing up, and next year I'm going to middle school." They get so full of themselves that they even get sassy. "What do you mean I can't have 'computer' in two of my squares!"

"No, just one."

Power is something they feel. They see themselves moving, being efficient, being grown-up. So if sometimes this gets to be heady stuff because we "really are equal partners," then I understand, even while I'm taking them down a notch or two.

One time a few of them headed down to the principal's office and proclaimed, "We really have to have a school dance." The principal later said to me: "For every argument presented, they shot one back. What have you done to them up there?" I suppose that what I had done was to let the energy loose.

Every year there are probably two to five children who do not accept the whole idea of a powerful self. For one reason or another, they do not catch the prevailing spirit. Quietly—even politely—they resist. JoAnn, I remember, dawdled through her morning assignments, managing to finish just before lunch, leaving little time for contract work. Kimberly came to school for friends and recess, spending her time being pleasant but wanting no part of "extra work." Robbie had spent his school life "bothering others," so contract time gave him an additional opportunity to indulge in that sport. Bill had a one-track approach to problems and puzzlers. There was only one answer, which he had to find in a few seconds or the task was not worth doing. He dismissed a crossword puzzle needing a three-letter word when the one he knew was right had five letters. He didn't want help, he didn't want clues, he didn't want to do it if his first answer wasn't right.

Elaine was a gifted child who had always gone home with good grades, but she liked to do what she liked to do. Anything else, including Mindwinders and the tough math questions I was putting on her contracts, she called "boring." When she finished her assignments, she liked to draw pictures, chat with friends, perhaps read a little. School was supposed to be easy. It had always been easy. As she saw the situation, she didn't have to work to stay at the top of the class because it was her rightful place. It really bothered her that Julie, whom she knew from third and fourth grade and who always had had academic problems, was far ahead of her in completed contracts, earning "good" or "very good" on her report card. During the second semester, when Elaine and Julie were seated at the same table, I'd hear Julie say, "Need help, Elaine?" They began to work together and became good friends.

In the end, based on the number of contracts she had completed, Elaine earned a report-card grade of *S* in independent work: *S* for satisfactory, not *E* for excellent, and not *G* for good. Among the gifted children, some like to work hard, taking risks even if occasionally they feel muddled. Some, like Elaine, want to stay with what's safe. I'd have to lump Elaine with those few other children who said to themselves about contracts: "I'm only doing this because she makes me."

Suzie I knew this class. Each of these children was Everychild. All of them were my children. As a parent who had seen three children through adolescence, I wished there had been a training ground for managing work in their fifth-grade year before they hit the combat zones in junior high and beyond. Once they left elementary school, they saw not one but several teachers. Each brought home several assignment sheets and schedules for work due, not to mention a blizzard of announcements about extracurricular activities. At home I wanted to help sort out the papers and the binder, but I was never sure how much oversight was too much.

"What do parents say about contracts?" I asked Suzanne.

Suzanne Parents can be apprehensive, especially when I say I don't have deadlines for contracts and explain how this policy is deliberately different from reading and math, for which I make set assignments every day. I once had a parent demand that I tell her child exactly what to do (this business of choice was preposterous) and to make sure he got it done on time. "No," I said, "this is the time to make clear to your child that only he—not me and not you—has charge of his time and his work pace."

On parents' night, I talk about pace, which is a key word in terms of personal responsibility. "The pieces of work are short enough," I tell the parents, "that the child can finish a contract rather quickly and call it done. Over the course of the year, children might finish anywhere from fifteen to thirty-five contracts. Pace becomes obvious in the way that pace is obvious for a swimmer: It's easily measured, and children become aware of it. They stand back and see their movement. They can control both the order of the tasks and the speed at which they work."

What makes the element of pace interesting is the rule that contracts cannot be taken home and cannot be done after school or in the lunch hour. Contract work is allowed only in the morning when the writing, reading, and math are finished. There's no rushing through these assignments either, since this is work that has to be done acceptably and, in the case of math, handed in before lunch. Since I'm the one making out new contracts, I gain a clear idea not only about who gets contracts finished but how much time each child takes with math and reading.

The children get used to the idea that I will be sitting at my desk during contract time, expecting contracts to be handed in and preparing to comment. Each time a child turns in a contract, I observe the date on which it was begun, write down the date on which it's being turned in, and take note of the time it took to finish. "Only a week. You're marching along," I say. Or, with a note of disbelief, I may say, "Three weeks? What took so long?" My words are not accusing, but they do require an explanation from the child.

The first response to such a question usually is "I dunno" or no answer at all. But I wait, and eventually the answer comes: "I took a long time on math," or "I was messing around." The contract in front of us, which shows evidence of work accomplished as well as the pace at which the work was done, evokes the same sort of discussion as the "what I did" column in the child's goals folder during writing hour. Is there a problem? If a problem is being hidden, it will probably be revealed during this short exchange.

"You decided to mess around instead of working on your contract?" The nature of, reasons for, and results of messing around make up the conversation that follows. In these conversations I almost always use the words *decide* and *decision* because I want the children to think of themselves as people who operate independently of the teacher's authority during the contract hour. People who "decide" tell *themselves* when to work. They take on that responsibility.

Suzie   What do you say to the parents of the children who have the most problem with contracts?

Suzanne   I suggest to all the parents—not just to those of a JoAnn, a Kimberly, a Robbie, or a Bill—that they have the same conversation with the child when the contract comes home that I had with the child when the contract was turned in. Look at the time elapsed between beginning and finishing, I suggest, then applaud the diligent effort or ask, "What took so long?"

What happens with most dawdlers after one of these conversations is that they work industriously for one or two contracts, then begin to lag again. They really need to know that everyone is pulling for them. They need a cheering section.

I remember one parent who, in trying to be helpful, suggested that I send the contract home for homework. "But if it goes home," I replied, "then I defeat one of the important purposes of the contract, which is to promote awareness of pace in school. It would make it too easy for the child to think, 'Well, I don't really have to do this now.'"

Suzie   What do you say to parents, then, about homework?

Suzanne   Homework is a story in itself. It should be told here because, like the contracts, it emphasizes time management. However, because it's so central to the whole relationship between school and home, it weaves itself into the overall plan for the classroom in a number of ways.

Homework is an important word on the school scene because it marks the spot where school and home interact and sometimes collide. When sparks fly, homework is often the point of friction: between child and parent, between child and teacher, and sometimes between teacher and parent.

"Don't you have any homework?" asks the parent, who then questions the teacher. "He tells me that he never has any homework. He says he gets it done in school. Would you please send me a note? I never know what he's supposed to do."

Or a parent might say, "He's supposed to do math, but he can't remember to bring the book home."

Children can do a power thing with their parents, manipulating them with words and looks that say: "Stop doing what you're doing so you can help me." Homework time is sometimes the occasion when deep-seated problems between parent and child erupt, since homework is something the child was "sposta" do and did not.

Back in the days when I allowed the children to finish their lessons at home, I invariably had trouble the next day. "Oh, I can't do my math because my math book's at home," somebody would say. Some children figured out that since I allowed them to talk to one another during class and also let them take their classwork home, they might as well do their assignments at home and spend their time at school playing. Some got into the habit of thinking, "I'll take this home, and Mom will sit next to me, and we'll do it together," or even, "Mom will do it."

Given the choice, I might have done away with homework entirely and given extra credit for the reading and such that the children did at home, but there was no way I could do this. In my community, homework is a given. My school district has a policy that every child at the age of ten should do no less than forty-five minutes of homework per night. So I devised a plan that I hoped would turn a negative into a positive. I redefined the word *homework*.

"Homework," I told the children, "is work of the kind you do in school, which makes you smart, clever, and intelligent. The only difference is that you do it at home."

"Realize," I continued, "that you get out at 2:15 when people are still working. There are more things that you need to know than we have time for in school, so you need to keep learning after you leave. You do that even now. You don't stop learning when you walk out the door."

"I'll give you assigned homework," I said, "but it will not take you the whole forty-five minutes every night. After you've finished it, you'll decide what to do to help yourself learn. These other things, like all the reading you do, you can count as homework. Just put the title and author of the books you read on your personal reading record and keep the record in your homework envelope."

The children do a significant amount of reading at home and enter the titles they have read on the personal reading record contained in the homework envelope (see Figure 10–3). When I last counted, the average number of books read at home over the year was twenty-two per child (counting "skinny books" as one-half each). The number per child ranged from 106 to 6.

The assigned homework is different from the work done in school, though it complements ongoing lessons. I always ask the

MY PERSONAL READING RECORD

Title and Author

Kind of Book: fantasy, adventure, mystery, historical fiction, fiction set in modern times, science fiction, biography, poetry, animal or science book, folk tales, other.

FIGURE 10–3   A Copy of the Record for Reading at Home

children to read the *Weekly Reader* and to watch television news or read the newspaper, so we can talk about current happenings. When we do the brain unit, I ask them to write notes about their dreams. If a problem has surfaced for a particular child—for example, long division—then I assign individualized homework. The child who receives this assignment has no more than the others in the class, only different homework.

I tell the children, "The lessons you do in school you don't take home. Those stay here."

And I emphasize, "Homework is your work, not your parents' work and not my work. I did fifth grade already, so I did that work, and your parents have done fifth grade, so they've done theirs. This is your work because you are the one doing fifth grade."

"I give you a grade on homework," I say. "I expect you to do acceptable work and learn how to plan and manage your time." At this point, I turn the district's forty-five minute policy into a time-management and math problem. "You'll have your homework envelope at home for nearly a week," I say, "from Monday afternoon until Friday morning when you bring it back. At forty-five minutes per night, and four nights a week, how many minutes would that be for each week's homework?"

The children keep track of what they do and the time they spend each night, then they add up their minutes for the week. Their parents sign the schedule, and the children return it to me just once a week (see Figure 10–4). (When they begin averaging in math, they work out the average for each night as well.) They earn a check mark for doing the minimum, a check plus for doing more, a plus for more than that. They earn a check minus for doing less than the minimum, and a zero, which is less than check minus, for forgetting to bring the envelope. All of these are evaluations that eventually are converted to a report-card grade. So the children's challenge is partly how to manage time and partly how to be in charge of remembering things.

On Friday mornings in September I'm likely to hear, "Oh, dear, my Mom forgot to put out my envelope."

"This is not Mom's homework," I'll say.

Homework schedule for _Shaun_

Week of _Sep. 14–18_

5th grade-45 minutes minimum daily
Required homework: _Weekly Reader_
Enrichment Worksheet 6 – Roman Numerals
Team Poster
Audubon Adventures

Start to find out where your ancestors came from – countries and continents

Monday (125)
35 min. – Team Poster
30 min. – Weekly Reader
10 min. – EWG
15 min. – Audubon Adventures
35 min. – Drackenberg Adventure chap. 4-8

Tuesday (65)
15 min. – letter
10 min. – Read, Spooks pg. 1-30 finished
40 min. – Read, The Drackenberg Adventure chap 9-12

Wednesday (80)
80 minutes – Made Junior pinball machine

Thursday (90)
(90) min. – Made another game

Parent Comments:

Parent signature _J. M. Mahney_

45) 360
90

Total time (minutes)
360

FIGURE 10–4   A Homework Schedule, Filled Out and Signed

"I had soccer practice yesterday, so I didn't get it done."

"Don't wait until the last minute," I'll say. "You never know what will happen on Thursday."

On Monday, when I hand back the envelope with the new week's homework, someone will say, "Why'd you give me check minus? I did all the work you gave me. It didn't take forty-five minutes."

"Then you need to count all the work you do at home that helps you become smart, clever, and intelligent. Think about that. You owe me a full forty-five minutes."

Taking personal responsibility for learning requires that they be alert and aware of available learning opportunities. I encourage them to think again about what might count for homework time. As time passes, they come in with suggestions, redefining homework as the work they do at home.

"Could I count cleaning my room?"

"I don't think so."

"Could I count my piano lessons?"

"Once a week," I say.

"Could I count my birthday party?"

"Why?" I ask.

"Because I made the invitations. I made a budget. I planned the refreshments and the games, and then I wrote thank-you notes."

"Sure."

"Does baking a cake count?"

"What are you learning when you do that?"

"I have to measure things, like a quarter of something, and that's math."

"That sounds good to me."

Suzie   I looked in awe at the sheer amount of detail Suzanne was handling. How many children in the class? twenty-seven? more often thirty? There were both the homework envelope to deal with and the contract, with each contract containing twelve boxes. Assuming an average of twenty contracts per child and twenty-seven children, a total of 540 contracts were being issued each year. This meant that between three and four contracts either were being negotiated or collected (upon completion) every single day. Then there was the checking off of each completed item—the "signing." Even with an aide, could this be done in the contract hour?

"How do you get the time?" I asked. "I honestly don't see how you do this. Do you take the contracts home to check over?"

Suzanne Both contracts and homework probably seem more complicated than they are. I don't aim to work myself into the grave. After school I read a few reading response logs and correct all the math spirals, but except for the homework envelopes once a week, I take nothing home. As for the contracts, I keep the puzzles and problems on shelves or in a filing cabinet near my desk so they are ready for making new ones. I can make out new contracts, give clues, and collect the finished ones during the contract hour. With an aide or a parent working at the opposite end of the room on the checking, helping with corrections, and signing, I can get it all done, though children may have to wait for an available signer.

The children work well with any volunteer who comes in. Sometimes I'll have adults in the room who I didn't even realize were there. A child will bring a contract to me and it'll be signed "D.R.S., 4–20," and I'll say, "Who was that?"

"Oh," they say, "that was the guy that was delivering paper," or "That was Mary Alice's mother who brought her her lunch." Once I had a wonderful principal who happened to be very tiny, and sometimes I'd see her initials on contracts when I didn't know at all that she had paid a visit. "Hmmmmm," I'd think, "I wonder what I was doing."

Parents are important signers. I'll pass this message along through the children: "We need some mothers and dads, or grandmas or grandpas, to come in and sign contracts." Most of the mothers work, and it's hard for them, but some drop in once or several times. It's only an hour.

Having parents come in to sign contracts is a nice way of having them in the room. Teachers are sometimes reluctant to have parents come in as aides because when they arrive, the teachers have to stop in the middle of what they're doing to explain what to do. But signing is a tidy job. I don't have to do any explaining since either the children or the answer books can do that. It's especially good if a child is having trouble in the class because the parent, rather than "observing," is accomplishing something. The child is happy that Mom or Dad has come to help, and the parent gets a good idea of how the child is getting along.

The adults give me valuable feedback. Esther Chambers, a volunteer for many years though not a parent, tells me about helping Tim correct his Monster Math. "He still needs work on multiplication facts," she tells me. I make a note of it.

If I have no one to sign contracts, things get a little rough because then I must sign them myself, and I cannot use the contract hour to sit with the children and make out new ones. Usually I'll do between two and five new contracts each day, but if I can't do that and someone says, "I need a new one," then I say, "Go ahead on the next Mindwinder or the next Super Sum, and I'll put that on your next contract when we make it out." Things go better when I have parents sign contracts.

As far as time goes, one of the most important advantages of the contract is the flexibility it adds to the whole morning schedule. Because contract time is the last hour of the morning, the children can use some of the hour to finish their reading or math. Therefore, I have leeway in the schedule to allow a child, within limits, to move ahead or work more slowly than the others. At the same time, no one is allowed to believe they have free-choice time, which for most children is perceived as indoor recess. The flexibility in the schedule allows me, in turn, to insist that everyone finish up their work before going to lunch. I can therefore require personal responsibility.

Suzie When Suzanne first talked to me about contracts as a lesson in individual responsibility, I thought she meant that children worked alone. She soon straightened me out on that. Children helped one another at their tables, she said. Being independent and personally responsible had nothing to do with working alone. But it had everything to do with the self.

The point about the sense of self came up in the middle of writing this chapter, when Suzanne and I sat down and talked about the chapter with other teachers. "Now that I see the whole picture," said one of the teachers, "I see that you really do control."

Suzanne demurred.

"I mean, in the end you clearly direct their efforts toward goals you have for them."

"Well, sure."

"You're pushing them. The contract and the homework both are ways to make them do a whole lot beyond the standards of fifth grade. You've got everything designed to make them go where you want them to go."

"I'll buy that," I said. "You really do push."

Suzanne   The choice of words is wrong. I don't "make them." The children know that I make them finish their math spirals before lunch, make them take off their baseball caps inside the room, and, in fact, make them do all sorts of things. But they also know that none of these rules are arbitrary; they're what any member of a community would expect if the community is to work smoothly. The children know, for example, that I need to correct the math spirals before I plan the next day's lessons.

As for pushing them, I don't think the children see me in that role. They apparently accept the idea I've offered at the beginning of the year and which I keep on building as the year progresses—the idea that they really are powerful because they have powerful brains. They see themselves as the ones who do the pushing. That's their image of themselves.

That image of the self is developed by the contract. The contract demonstrates what great things the brain is capable of. First, it's inventive and purposeful. It can think of things to do that will aid learning. Second, it gets things finished and regulates pace. Third, it looks back, finds mistakes, and corrects them. It even finds the problems behind the mistakes.

On all of those points the contract and the homework put me in touch with each child individually. Both the homework schedule and the contract provide space for the child's choices. Both require that the child say to me: "Here's how long it took me," and in some cases, "Here's why it took me that time." Finally, both provide a way for the child to deal with mistakes—to identify and learn from them—so that these corrections are neither "extra work" nor punishment.

Suzie "You've got them nailed," said one of the teachers with obvious admiration. We all had a laugh. In this class there was no escaping responsibility and no hiding—not for a single soul. Likewise, there was no escaping the conclusion that powerful brains naturally work hard.

ELEVEN

....

Scaffolding a Social Ethic

Suzie   In the morning, sitting in Suzanne's classroom, I had seen Betsy and Santo working on their contracts. In the afternoon I saw them in their simulation game, *Pioneers* (Wesley 1974). They wore nametags showing the names of real people who had made the difficult journey westward across the Rockies—Dr. Joseph Mingo and Elizabeth Swanson. Their wagon train was one of four in the class.

    The contracts taught individual responsibility. The wagon train unit taught a group ethic. The two parts of the curriculum, the individual and the group, were mutually supportive, each contributing to the success of the other. The group ethic was the ultimate goal of the classroom and individual responsibility a means of attaining that goal.

The writing groups and book groups we talked about earlier in this book were opportunities for playing out social roles and learning social responsibilities. This chapter says more about playing roles and practicing the parts, but now we turn to the social ethic as an explicit idea. We turn to social studies, that area of the curriculum that provides a bridge between a self in interaction with a small group and a self in interaction with histories and cultures.

The two children closest to me were in conversation. Julie (in the role of Samantha Wilson) had not finished lightening her wagon the day before, so it was still too heavy to cross the Sand Flats River. Now she had to consider which supplies to throw over the side to reduce the weight. If she did not, the whole wagon train, which was waiting for her, would be delayed. The travellers couldn't leave her to face the dangers alone. They had to stick with her and help her solve her problem. Then, together, they could be on their way toward Oregon, their final destination.

Suzanne   The *Pioneers* game tells the children what roles they'll play and what problems they'll face along the trail. The children improvise the language and play out the problem situations on their own.

By recreating the past, these children try out their futures. They play the roles of people who face danger and hardship, pull together, grieve for one another's losses, and make decisions about how to survive. Thinking now has a social dimension. The children work for the common good.

Suzie   Working for the common good is an ideal I associate with the Greeks. In the ancient books, virtue was civic virtue, having a public meaning rather than a private one. A good person, a virtuous student, looked to the health of the state. I think of togas and laurel wreaths, men raising their arms as they made impassioned but rational speeches to the citizens of the Greek city states, urging them to one course of action or another. I realize that in Greece women and slaves had little chance of attaining this particular brand of virtue, not to mention the fact that the common good everybody would have been most interested in achieving was military victory. The survival of the known civilization in those days depended on it.

Never mind. Times are different now, and the common good is still the most legitimate goal of learning. Inviting women and slaves into the discourse (for slaves of a sort are still on the scene) and removing the threat of the extinction of human civilization from the forefront of our thinking ought to make it possible to redefine the common good. Needed for this process of redefinition are articulate and committed people. The Greeks' basic assumption still holds true: the final goal of learning is civic. A good learner looks to the health of the society as a whole, raising her voice, his voice, to urge the making of wise choices.

Suzanne   The group ethic of the *Pioneers* wagon train is to think of your own wagon in terms of what it means for the men, women, and children in the entire line of wagons. By spring, when I begin the wagon train game, the connection between individual responsibility and the common good is something the children have begun to grasp. Consequently, they enter the role playing with a good understanding of what it means to contribute to a group effort, to listen to the problems of others, to help, and so on. By the spring they have also acquired a sense that history is alive with people. Their idea of "the past" has been fleshed out, their stock of concepts for describing large movements—for example, revolutions—and geographical space—countries and continents—has been greatly enlarged. By spring, Betsy and Santo, playing Mrs. Swanson and Dr. Mingo, regard the westward journey as a metaphor for group struggle.

As in previous chapters, I talk here about scaffolds, the procedural methods I use to invite children to join in and do while I wait for them to gain consciousness and sense of purpose. The consciousness I work toward is still that of a self with a powerful brain, but in this case a self whose powerful brain leads the children to have an impact on the groups of which they are a part.

Suzie   One of the most obvious ways to have an impact on a group is to make a contribution, thereby making the self a valued member. I learned, when I talked to Suzanne about contracts and homework in the last chapter, that every time a child finished a contract, that child contributed five hundred points to the total for the team. If the child earned a "plus" for the weekly homework, that added another five hundred points. Thus, the reward for individual effort was more than self-satisfaction; the team loved the member who worked.

Karen Watson-Gegeo, a member of my HART research group in Honolulu, used to tell stories of children in the Solomon Islands, who learned in the traditional way, from family members and other villagers. Karen was impressed with the effectiveness of this traditional system of education, seeing the incredible skill of three-, four-, and five-year-olds in such survival abilities as gardening and finding food in the forest. Toddlers were inspired to work hard, she noted, by the continuing message that their work contributed directly to the family. Even the smallest bit of food found and brought to the house by a small child was enough to evoke lavish praise from parents and siblings. The consequent sense of personal responsibility was remarkable, said Karen.

Each of us in HART brought with us the insights we had gathered from our various academic disciplines. These insights we contributed to the group, together with various kinds of studies—with university students, with toddlers, and with children of Hawaiian and Pacific island ancestry.

Suzanne   Contributing to the common good is something the children do in a very tangible way when they bring and make a gift of their individually earned points to their teams. They know about teams because they are part of the history of the classroom. The posters made by teams in earlier years and displayed high on the wall above the chalkboard remind them of their part in a long tradition. I talk in mystical tones about the spirit of past classes still lingering in our room. As with the great academic institutions—with their gargoyles, their hallowed halls, and their sense of the past—the very space we sit in is imbued with the expectation that every child will enter in and contribute.

Of all the groups, including the writing group, the book groups, and eventually the wagon trains, the team is the group to which the children contribute most often and most visibly. When I want to call attention to group spirit, I'll say, "When I came in this morning, all the chairs were down. Each of you give yourself one hundred points." Or I'll say, "Maria, I see you working particularly well with Kimmie. Give yourselves 250 points." Or I'll call attention to the mere fact that we're all together, all struggling: "This is really a hot day, and we are all dead tired. Everybody gets fifty points." I tell substitute teachers, "Feel free to give points." I may give one thousand points to the first team that agrees to an answer on a math strategy problem that turns out to be right, then seven hundred points to the next team, and so on.

The first thing each morning, I put a proofreading exercise on the chalkboard; the teams have to decide how to repair the errors. When I signal one of the teams, the chairperson of that team comes to the board and repairs the sentence, then looks around at the class to see if another team has challenged. If there's a challenge, it has to be resolved, and the winning team—either challenger or defender—gets points. "Five hundred points for the Fabulous Five," I'll say, and then the chairperson of the Fabulous Five has to add those points to the team's running total.

The rewards for winning at the end of the semester are pretty skimpy. The winners get little certificates that read "High honors for cooperation in your team"; the others get certificates that say "Honors." Each time they select books for the book groups, the members of the team with the most points at that moment get first choice of the new books. But the team members with first choice select different books, so it can hardly be said that they're out to win a particular book. The prize at the end is not the central attraction. Points are fun, that's all.

It's the team chairperson's job to keep the numbers straight; all I do is collect the total at the end of each week. Actually, some chairpersons do a terrible job of keeping the points. They lose them or add them up wrong, especially when the numbers approach fifty and sixty thousand. Doing the accounts turns out to be a team project in itself. But the team project is where the children's attention goes. They don't get wrapped up in thoughts of a prize or reward.

Suzie The team is a kind of family, the way the Solomon Islanders are families. One nonworking member can throw the whole unit out of kilter. You say the children don't get wrapped up in the final reward, but they must look at the Joneses next door and say, "Why aren't we up there with them? Why don't you start contributing?"

Suzanne They're bothered if they think their team is last. Sometimes I'll hear a team member say, "We are going to be totally embarrassed." The members of Patti's team came to me because they were losing team points, and it was "her fault." Here was a problem of personal responsibility. That's when we started the discussion "What to do about Patti?"

Patti was chatty, and perky, and cheerful, but she never did her homework, never contributed homework points. In fact, when she didn't have her homework envelope at all on Friday morning, she was *minus* five hundred points. She also lost things. "Oh, gosh," she'd say, "I did that, but who knows where it is? It's gone." So I said to the team when Patti wasn't present, "All right, those are things that are a problem for Patti. How can you help her as a team?"

Well, the children had no idea. This was the teacher's job. I was supposed to speak to Patti and shape her up. I knew that they went over to one another's houses, and they knew what was going on, so I said, "Why do you suppose she isn't getting her homework done?"

"She gets locked out of the house after school," said one team member.

So then I said, "That's a real problem. Could she come over to someone else's house and do her homework?"

"Well, that's an idea," someone said.

And then about losing things, I said, "Well, you know, she's terribly disorganized in her desk and maybe it would be helpful when you're handing out papers to be sure she gets one and if things fall out of her desk, pick them up and hand them to her and say, 'Patti, this is important,' that sort of thing. Maybe she needs these extra hints."

Then later, when Patti came back, I said, "The team tells me you're having a problem with homework. How would you like someone to do homework with?" And then I let the whole matter go from there. I just kept my eye on how things were developing.

If it's a problem that only I can deal with, then I do. But I won't say, "Patti, you will NOT lose your papers. Patti, you will do your homework because the team wants you to." If it's a team problem, then it's the team's business.

As things turned out, Patti found that she could go home after school with Kay, which she did sometimes. But then she started going over to a neighbor's house and doing her homework there, so she saw that she could find solutions for herself. She stopped thinking, "Oh, heck, I don't do homework." Her team members were pretty pleased with her.

Suzie   If they need reminders, you're not the one to provide. You're not these children's mother.

Suzanne   I'm not their mother, and I don't own their problems.

Suzie   The team experience is a scaffold, isn't it, to enable children to learn how to work things out among themselves rather than calling on the higher authority to solve the problem.

Suzanne   It's a scaffold for learning a whole variety of ways to be socially responsive. As team members, the children start looking outside themselves. Often they've been self-centered, unnurturing, unable to affect anything or anyone beside their own sisters, brothers, mothers, or fathers. They haven't learned how to help—how to offer help or carry out the help in a way that others can appreciate.

So one thing I do is scaffold a helping routine, starting on the first day of school when I pass out the first contract. I say to the children, "Since everyone here is going to teach others, you need to learn how to give help." Then I show them how to help another child, using the first few items of the contract as examples. As with every instance of scaffolding, I have to make it easy for them to participate and make it very obvious what I'm calling this activity. "What we're doing here is helping, and one way to help is to give clues."

I then direct them to the word search located under the cover-sheet of the contract. The word search is an activity that asks them to find the name of every classmate hidden among the letters. This is a case where each child knows some but not all of the children in the class, so the game doubles as a get-to-know-your-classmates game. "Suppose," I tell them, "that you want to give someone at your table a clue, and suppose that person has found the name of everyone in the class but two. A clue would be that both names are on vertical lines and one is spelled backward."

"Helping is not cheating," I say. "Cheating is giving someone the answer, but if you help someone, you say things or draw on paper in such a way that the person finds the answer. When you give clues or ask them questions, then the other person can use their brain to get closer and closer to the answer, like a detective."

"You may give as many clues as you think appropriate," I say, "and I will give clues too, but only three on a task." (Clues are not to be wasted.)

There are more ways to help. "If someone asks you how to do something, your reply should be, 'What do you think you're supposed to do?' You can't start to help unless the person you're helping has already done some thinking. That person has to put in some effort first. If that person has read the directions, and then tried something that didn't work, you will know where to start to help."

Cheating is something the children know about. Unless I distinguish right away between cheating and helping, then they're confused about working in groups when I'm not there. They think, "Isn't this cheating when I talk to someone about my work?"

<u>Suzie</u>   Do you see real cheating?

Suzanne   Once in a great while, from a child who feels completely and utterly powerless in one part of life and has learned, through cheating, to be powerful in another. I remember a child named Arthur. He was a child whose family did everything for him. "You guys have all these chores. Not me, boy, I've got the best life of anybody." He did nothing without help; the school helped him, his mother helped him, his grandmother and grandfather helped him. He came to school one day with his homework written in his mother's handwriting. "I was too tired to do it," he said.

In school, Arthur manipulated everybody, including the aides and the other kids. He had a vast repertoire of strategies for getting other people to do the things he didn't know how to do. He would get sick, or he would flatter the dickens out of people, which is what he did to me. He took three-day weekends to care for a mysterious cough that his mother told me they were having investigated but couldn't find the cause of.

He also did a whole lot of real cheating. If he cheated while taking a test, I would pick up his paper, hand him a new one, then move his seat. But mostly the children worked together, helping one another, so, as far as I knew, the opportunities for real cheating were few.

I thought I pretty well had Arthur's number. I thought that, in spite of himself, he could hardly keep from learning because he was in contact with the supportive children in the groups.

Then one day—it must have been a Friday or Monday—Arthur was out. With a degree of sarcasm that I usually am able to control, I said, "Welllll, I suppose he has his cough." There was this stunned silence. In fact, it was so freezingly quiet in the room that I looked up from the roll sheet wondering what had happened. The children were looking at one another. You could hear them thinking. You could see the question in their eyes: "Should we say something?" It was a group look. Then, suddenly, hands shot up. People don't generally raise hands when they want to say something, so this was strange. I figured later that no one wanted to be the first to talk, but clearly the children wanted to be called on and required to talk.

"Mrs. Brady," someone said, "did you know that cough is a fake cough for whenever he doesn't want to go to school? He does it on purpose, then he brags about it. He stays home and watches TV in the morning, then he goes shopping with his mother in the afternoon." The feeling behind the question could scarcely be concealed: "Do you know the *vast duplicity* that has been visited upon this school?"

I wasn't surprised, but I didn't say so. I looked suitably shocked.

"And," said another child, "did you know that he bullies us if we're helping, if we give him clues but not the answer? He says, 'I'm going to beat you up at recess, and I'm going to beat you up after school.'"

I was now genuinely shocked. "Has he ever beaten anybody up?"

"No," others acknowledged. "He probably wouldn't."

"But," said another, "you're not supposed to say you're gonna beat someone up."

"He's twice as big as any other kid. He'll twist your arm until it hurts. He could just *sit* on you and break a few bones."

He had made Keith tell him the answer to the third problem on the math test. He made him come to the water fountain at the back of the room.

I thought to myself, "He is working this at a much deeper level than I was giving him credit for." So I said, "This sounds like my business, not just the team's business," and the children all said, "Yes, you have to do something."

Then the situation turned comical. We all in our ways liked Arthur. "Should we shoot him? Hang him?"

"Tell his mother," said someone. But several children said, "His mother won't do anything. He gets away with murder."

"You better write him a letter," said another child.

"OK," I answered. "What shall I say?" I wrote on the board *I have heard these things, I am disappointed, serious consequences will occur.* I wrote a draft and read it to the children in the afternoon. But they said it wasn't nearly strong enough, so I rewrote it. Then I said: "This is my letter, but if you would like to sign it, I'll leave it here on the table." I think every child signed.

I addressed it to Arthur, put it in the mail, and he got it before he returned to school. The day he came back, he came in the classroom, looked at the faces staring at him, and delivered one of his funny lines. "Whooooooa," he said in his deep, slow way of talking, "I shoulda been here." People laughed.

I said, "Arthur, we find this serious business, so if you want to stay in this class, you have to try harder. We have two other fifth grades. You can start all over again in another fifth grade. If you want to stay in this class, you'll have to change. Everyone is upset with you."

"Oh," he said, "I thought you guys were my friends."

"That's what friends do. Friends see when people are heading down the wrong track and try to help them."

Suzie   Did he improve? What happened in the end?

Suzanne   You never know what happens in the end. That's the trouble with having them at this age. They go off, and sometimes you just don't hear. Arthur stopped making people in the class tell him answers, but he was at heart so scared of failure that he would try practically nothing. I only hoped that he could get into a career that required charm alone.

Suzie   The other children, though, learned something about standing up against abuse. They complained, or they saw how others complained, then they did something about it.

Suzanne   It was a lesson, I suppose, in group responsibility. What some of the children saw and articulated for the others was that Arthur's cheating was their business. What he was doing was tearing at the social fabric, and they were deeply offended. In their language, it was just not fair. Ten-year-olds are passionately interested in what's fair and not fair; they'll talk on and on about the rules of a playground game. The same goes for the classroom, where they saw Arthur's strong-arm tactics, which were covered up and kept secret from me, as a terrible violation of the rules. They were working for a common good and he was working only for Arthur. More than personal injury was at stake. At stake were the rules themselves. Like all children, they were reluctant to tell because they wanted to think that they could run their world entirely without help. But eventually they saw that Arthur was threatening not just one but many. More than that, he had bamboozled even me, the higher authority, whose role, in their eyes, was to ensure that rules are followed. They were furious.

Their fury and their passion are typical of children of their age, but it's also typical that they would rather ostracize the wrongdoer than tell that person what they find offensive. The discussion in class took them through a process of saying, "Here's what we don't like." I needed to make sure that Arthur was given a way to come back and that the children saw me giving him this way.

Suzie So you see that the lesson learned was that group problems ought to be confronted and that people should use their voices or use their writing to do that.

Suzanne Certainly, though this was a lesson I hope I won't have to teach again in just this way.

Suzie Using the voice and using the pen were ways to grasp the problem in the first place. Students, if they see social problems at all, typically see them as distant and disembodied. Without talk, students fail to see them for what they are, even the close-up problems. In the year of the Rodney King beating case in Los Angeles, in a newspaper story that one of my freshman students brought in, students found meaning in the words *injustice* and *alienation* in the act of asking one another questions. As they talked, their posture changed. Their whole bodies looked more active. Their thinking had a very physical quality, as though their talking were a stimulant of some sort, turning up the pace of their thinking.

Suzanne

Children can tell themselves to wake up their minds, which is something I connect with the whole spirit of the team. They owe it to their team, and the team, in turn, owes it to the spirit of the classroom, to be active.

My campaign against passivity is another part of the scaffold for teaching a group ethic. On one of the first days in the year, I call attention to the poster on the door, which has the phrase NO LUMPS ON LOGS emblazoned right under BE SMART, CLEVER, AND INTELLIGENT. At the same time, I invoke the history of the classroom. I call on the helping spirit of all of those students who sat in these desks in prior years. I say, "Last year, when everyone in here was about to leave Monte Vista and go to middle school, I asked them to make these posters for you. This is what somebody wrote: *No Lumps on Logs.*"

Then I give my speech about what it means to be active. "It means that there is always thinking in your head. When we're having a discussion, and it's your turn to talk, you don't say, 'Well, I'll think about it,' because you've been thinking all along."

All of this emphasis on the activity of the mind is tied to the social obligation to be part of a team—to teach and help someone else.

Suzie

Particular phrases recurred in Suzanne's conversations about the social ethic, phrases that she used in speaking to the children. One was "helping someone." Another was "what's fair?" Others were "solving this problem," and "deciding," and "making a plan."

"You return to these words, don't you," I said one day. "I remember you did the same with *respond*, returning to it after the children had finished an activity and saying to them, 'So what does it mean to be a good responder?'" Children develop their abilities to judge and reflect by a continual process of redefinition (Bayer, Cognitive-Apprenticeship Learning, 1990). New experiences, especially those shared by their conversational partners, allow them to see a new slant on an old word. If they go back over the experience and say to themselves—or to a conversational partner—"was that fair?" then they develop a definition for that phrase that takes the experience into account. Their phrases, their tools for thinking, are thereby enriched. Consequently, when they encounter a new situation, they have an enriched vocabulary for thinking about that situation.

Suzanne   These words are a bridge for the children between their responsibilities as individuals and their responsibilities as social beings. The contract hour is mainly a time for individual responsibility, but the meanings for *decide* and *plan*, which they learn during that hour, stay with them when they go on to team projects, where they use those same words, plus the phrases "solving problems," "what's fair," and "how can you help?" This consciousness of themselves as people who "decide," and "solve," and "plan"—all this comes with them into the social context. Or maybe it works the other way: they acquire this consciousness during the team work, and then it comes with them into the individual work.

Then they bring that same consciousness with them into the social studies curriculum. One thing I do when we learn about the colonies and the American Revolution is to read to the children Jean Fritz' book *Can't You Make Them Behave, King George?* (1982). In this book, King George is a good father to the unruly children—the colonists. He has the best of intentions and can't understand why they are behaving so badly. The children laugh. They see the irony. Here's King George, angry and going into funks over the unruly behavior of his children when, of course, those unruly children are the honored forebears of the country. When we talk about the books written about the American Revolution from the colonists' point of view—for example, *April Morning* (Fast 1983)—someone will say, "What would King George say about that?" So what's fair takes on a new dimension.

Suzie   Do the children see "the common good" as "what's fair for everybody"? Is that the way they would see that?

Suzanne Yes, and a good decision, in the social context, is one that con-
tributes to greater fairness. They like the story about George Washington, how people said to him, "You can be president as long as you
want to be," and he said, "No, that's not a good idea." He knew that
revolutionary figures too often get into power and just stay there.
Then there's no government of the people but a government of the
revolutionary leader's supporters. So would that be fair? No, that
would not be fair. The children like the fact that our present-day
laws and rules go back to those basic principles and to the people
who believed in them.

I've talked to them about former President Nixon, and why he
got in trouble, and how he resigned just as he was going to be im-
peached. People lie, I tell them, and people cheat, and people do awful things, but you're really not supposed to. People expect you to be
trustworthy.

Expectations have a lot to do with the running of the teams. People are always expected to do their best, and they don't always do
this. When they don't, the children expect me to be disappointed;
they know I expect better. I remember when a couple of children returned to visit me from middle school. When I asked how everybody
was doing, Ryan said, "You would really be disappointed in Will and
Florie, Mrs. Brady." Apparently, Will and Florie were not behaving
their best, and that behavior was seen by Ryan and his friend as a reflection on them and the class they had all been part of.

<u>Suzie</u> I could remember nothing from my own study of social studies in
school that connected the big teams—governments and such—with
the smaller teams of which I was a member—my family, my Girl
Scout troop, my friends on the block. I remember causes and effects
of war. I remember products of import and export. (Or at least I remember that I knew them until the test was over.) What I learned of
group struggle in American history—the people who endured those
struggles and either failed or succeeded—I learned from reading
narratives such as Rolvaag's *Giants in the Earth* (1991). I remember
the family's sod house, the bitter cold, the locusts, and especially the
family's do-or-die spirit. If I connected that family's struggle with

anything in my personal life, I must have done so quite unconsciously. I certainly never talked about such things in school.

Suzanne   This connection we're making between the children's joint effort on the team and their understanding of a broader social ethic is easiest for them to see when I begin with family. I put team effort together with projects that teach respect for one another's families and family origin. The first social studies project of the year—and this is also a lesson in countries and continents—is to gather up all the facts about the countries and continents of everybody's ancestors in the class. "Unless you're Native American," I say, "your family came from another country, maybe another continent, and maybe more than one. You can't say your family came from Ohio or Tennessee because at some point we were all immigrants. You might have to write to your grandmother and ask." When the children have completed the research, each team takes all the ancestor information for everybody in the class and decides how best to make a graph or a table that will depict our class's diversity. The teams get points for the clarity of their finished graph, and whether the labels were helpful and correct, and whether they spelled the names of the countries correctly.

Suzie   If individual team members can contribute to an intelligent decision about the way to make the graph or table, then the team benefits.

Suzanne   That link between teamwork and learning about American history is now, I'm glad to say, part of the *History-Social Science Framework for California Public Schools for the State of California* (1988). In so many words, the writers of these guidelines connect the word *democracy* with the kind of group work I have the children do. The guidelines state: "While the ability to work with others is an asset in any society, it is a requirement for citizenship in a democracy" (24). They also state that "civic competence requires the skills that make joint effort and effective cooperation possible" (24). I abhor the word *skills* because I see such a difference between "skills" and "responsibility." A person can learn skills and never learn responsibility. Besides, the word reminds me of all those years I had to do workbooks with the reading series. But the point is that children really do have to practice being cooperative. They have to speak the words and go through the motions—act the whole thing out.

Suzie   Public virtue is something to be practiced. It's an active quality, not a passive one.

Suzanne   Which is where the wagon train project comes in. Over time, as the children make their way toward Oregon, they act out all the ways of being socially responsive that we've talked about. They care. They mourn. They worry. And of course, they plan ahead, make decisions, and solve problems—all with the entire wagon train in mind. The wagon train simulation is a classic scaffold, a game in which children are invited to participate so that they may internalize the conversation of that game.

Suzie   Back in Suzanne's classroom, I saw the children dressed in old-fashioned clothing, having just finished their trail diaries. Wrote Diane: "I'm sort of having second thoughts about my family going on this wagon train. Maybe we shouldn't have gone in the first place." Wrote Charles: "God, I got shot in the arm, and it's really hard to tend my oxen, but my wife really helped." Having started the year as "Charles the ghost," the Charles in chapter 3 who folded his arms and pushed away his chair, Charles was by May speaking of people helping him as though it were entirely commonplace and natural. Now he responded, he listened, and he expected to give help back—all part of his teamwork role.

The children gathered together to hear Suzanne read from the book *Pioneers* about the trails from which they had to choose. Reason and logic were the name of the game. They first listened to the choices, then consulted one another, then wrote their own argument.

Suzanne announced the choices: "All right, you have just arrived at Fort Choice. There are three trails you can take. Trail A is the Lone Pine Trail, which goes by an Indian burial ground. The local Indians have attacked other wagon trains for disturbing their ancestors' graves, but actually that's the easiest route to take. Then there is Trail B, the Risky Trail; you may run out of water on this trail because we've heard that the water holes are dried up."

Then she described the hazards of Trail C. The children took notes, then turned the page of their learning log, and wrote their own analyses:

> Trail A would be good, but we've already lost our rifles in the last round and if we get attacked, it's the end. Trail B is better because we have lots of barrels of water and we could probably get through without having to fill up again, and besides we've lost a lot of our animals, so they don't need water anymore.

They got together with their wagon train and decided as a group what to do, negotiating from their differences of opinion. The wagon master then wrote up the group decision and attached it with a paper clip to all the individual written arguments. "Your points on these," said Suzanne, "will show whether your reasoning makes sense and whether your group decision took everyone's argument into consideration."

Suzanne   People ask me sometimes how I can evaluate achievement in social studies when the goals prescribed by the state are things like "ethical understanding," and the "capacity to make wise choices in their own lives," and "developing a keen sense of citizenship." How can anybody tell whether children have these understandings or do these things?

So what do I do? For one thing, I look at the response logs written by the children as they read historical fiction. A child who was wagonmaster of his wagon train, the one made especially responsible for the well-being of his group, now shows that sense of concern as he reads Laura Ingalls Wilder's *The Long Winter* (1971). He's got ideas about survival. If he'd been there himself, he would have had a plan.

> No wonder the story is called *The Long Winter*. If they are go-ing to have five more blizzards it will be a very long winter. I think they should all sleep in the same place so they could stack up the covers and not be cold.

This child's responses early in the year were reactions. They were not suggestions for how the characters might consider the welfare of the group.

Another child (Mrs. Brown from the wagon train) looks to the contributions made by family members to other family members:

> I'm glad that Pa finally let Laura help him. She can do the same things Pa does, so Pa has it a lot easier now. Mary is sweet for voltering her college money for the families needs. She puts her family ahead of her dreams.

The writer knows, as she writes, that Mary went to college in the end, but she finds that the conflict between personal achievement and family needs is something worth noting.

I also look at the number of children who become actively in-volved. This past year, when the three fifth-grade teachers (Marilyn, Ellen, and I) decided to coordinate our yearly play with the wagon train project and call it *Goin West,* eighty of the eighty-five children in the three classrooms wanted to have speaking or solo singing parts. What a contrast this was with past years, when not nearly as many of the children felt they belonged in center stage. The wagon train simulation made them feel that they belonged together; they played these roles to the hilt.

Suzie I noticed that same sense of belonging together in the children's written language. Suzanne showed me the children's written re-sponses to a request she had made of them. As she put this request to the children: "The substitute teacher told me that she needed to understand more about the atmosphere in this class. Since the chil-dren are teachers in this room, she wonders what the children expect to do, and also what she ought to do herself. So, if you were talking to her, what would you tell her to expect? What is the class-room atmosphere?"

In their answers to the substitute teacher, the children made it clear that they liked relying on each other rather than the teacher. Group reliance is what they were used to. The substitute should be careful not to tread on their communal sense of self.

In the written responses, which follow unedited, nearly every child used the word *self-directed*. The word was familiar to them, said Suzanne, because she used it when she talked to the children about going to middle school. The middle school always required a rating from her on each child's "self-directedness." Interestingly, to judge by the children's written responses, they had interpreted the word *self,* normally thought to be an individual person, as a group of people. The "self" was not "I" but "we." Sarah, for example, says: "Our class is usually self directed by this time of year. We usually always help other classmates when they need it." Says David: "Our classroom is noisy, but most of it is self-directed." Says Alison: "We are self-directed that means that we basicaly know what to do—on are own." Says Roy, a hyperactive child who cannot sit still without the help of his teammates: "We know what to do we don't need any help."

The commentaries show agreement both in terms of independence and group identity. Only Patti's comments stand out. Not quite getting the point about classroom atmosphere, she writes: "I think the room is quiet and smells OK. Sometimes the room smells good." Someone on the team must have helped her out. She draws a line through the comments about smelling, then she writes: "In the morning we write then read then do math then go out for recess after recess we do contracts and other things. And our class is self-Dericted. that is something." Patti knows where to turn for advice.

Suzanne The children feel such a bond to the people in the group that they find it natural to say, "We have a responsibility here" and "We need to talk about this." I remember the time a group of sixth graders who had been in the classroom a year earlier came back from middle school, right in the middle of our afternoon hour.

Everyone in their middle school had received a terrible fright. It seems a small group of boys brought a gun to school with a plan to kill another boy. They were not a gang, not kids with criminal records, but just kids. Unfortunately, not one of them would put the brakes on or tell someone. The intended victim stayed in at recess, and the plot fizzled, but the gun remained at school hidden away. The whole plan came to light when a child finally told a teacher, but by that time many children had learned about the gun and had remained silent. Our community was stunned—by the plot, by the weapon, and by the silence of those students.

So in the middle of the uproar, these five students from my previous year's fifth grade class showed up. They had early dismissal and hurried over the few blocks from their school. "We've come to talk to the fifth graders," they said. "We want to have a panel discussion." They pulled chairs over to the rug, a clear request for the class to come and listen. I was to come too.

Sheri was obviously in charge. She gave introductory comments and indicated who was to speak next. All five gave their own interpretations of the situation and spoke of the climate at the school. I realized they were not coming as reporters, but as the big kids returning to soothe the younger ones. "Don't be afraid to come to middle school" was their message. "It was stupid not to tell the adults. Those kids know that now." They felt confident that the adults who worked at the school were handling things well.

I was so proud of them. They cared. They acted. I remembered them the previous May "getting their families to Oregon;" writing diary entries as adults; and caring for old Grandma, "who was getting plumb wore out," and little Ben, who fell off the wagon and "needed tending."

Suzie   I thought again of the Greek orator raising his arm in an impassioned gesture before a great throng of listeners. That was the wrong image, I had now decided, for the "civic competence" we hoped to be teaching in schools. A more appropriate image was the seated conversationalist. Civic competence was so frequently a small-group act as opposed to speech making. It was talking face-to-face in a turn-taking style. It also had a nurturing quality that I was only late in life coming to see: it was all that ability to plan, to decide, to solve problems, and then bringing all of it to bear in the interests of the younger, the weaker, and those who depended on you.

"Do you think the children understand how complicated it is to figure out what the common good really is?" I asked Suzanne.

Suzanne   For now, they understand what's fair and what's not fair, and many of them who have never learned to be actively involved now act. They're ten and eleven years old, and they know that they have the power that a powerful brain can give them. For many of them, the lessons of the fifth grade are that they belong to groups who need that energy and intelligence, and that they have what it takes to help out.

TWELVE

Teachers in Conversation

Suzie In the previous chapters, Suzanne and I have looked together at children. Now we turn the lens around and look at ourselves. We've been talking so far about change—change in the way Suzanne teaches writing, changing away from the basal reader, and a change toward the creation of consciousness that results in a social ethic. Now we talk about what it takes to make that change.

Other books make the case for educational change at the level of the state legislature or the district board of education. We make the case in this chapter for change as teachers themselves make it. We say that teachers need what the children in Suzanne's classes need, the empowerment provided by a conversational atmosphere. Recall from the last chapter the effort undertaken by Patti and the others in the class to define the atmosphere of the class. Remember the typical response: "we're in this together . . . we help each other . . . we don't really like the idea of an authority telling us what to do all the time." Recall also the reason for doing this exercise, the substitute's remark "I'm not sure how to be a teacher in this room. Your class is different." That difference was the children's sense that people in their classroom had intelligences, in the plural, to share and swap with one another. In this chapter, we recognize that such an attitude toward learning is the source of empowerment. Turning now to teachers, we ask how it is possible to recognize those good swapping sessions, how to encourage them, and how to make them a systematic part of school life.

Suzanne   What teachers need, of course, is Suzie, a persistent voice in the ear who asks you why at every turn. That's what I loved about the ten-year conversation; it's what I need. It didn't hurt that Suzie was a university professor who was versed in the theory of language learning, and I suppose it was her university habits of mind that made her hang around for all these years and continue to ask questions, but the great benefit of conversing with her was that she was from somewhere else. She didn't know my school, nor had she ever taught elementary school. There were lots of things we had in common, but it was those differences—different intelligences, you could say—that made it perfectly logical for her to ask "Why are you doing that?" Then, of course, I had to face up to the question and ask, "Well, why *am* I doing this?"

There were other differences between us. During the summers we worked together, Suzie was up at 6:30 jogging around Carmel, ready with her best stuff before nine. By nine, I was just beginning to move my mouth and put sentences together. Then there were the ways in which she used writing. I tend to keep things in my head. She'd say, "Write that down." She'd be scribbling on yellow pads. "We can think about this later," she'd say, and then she did think about whatever it was later. She didn't let anything fly by. She caught it, thought it, classified it, rethought it, and maybe in in the end threw the whole thing out.

I was reminded of what I taught the kids as they observed themselves playing blocks: you can always build a better wall, so feel free to tear this one down. That's what Suzie did with the computer. She wrote umpteen versions, then ended up with one. I've always been one to go back and rethink things, but Suzie's habits taught me to have even more faith in that process. Over the years I've become more and more comfortable replacing one classroom activity with another because I feel, "Well, I've thought about it, and I can do this."

This brings me to the idea of authority, and the whole conversational atmosphere in which teachers make decisions about change in their classroom practices.

When I talk to groups of teachers about giving up the basal, the workbooks, or some traditional practice, I'm frequently asked, "How did you get by with that? Why did they let you do that?" It's the question of authority and where it comes from. What has helped me deal with this question in my own teaching is the thought that "they" are not the only people with whom I converse. I have Marilyn and Ellen in the same school. And I talk to Suzie.

I can remember my first real conversation of this kind. "Grace, what can I do? I promised these first graders that reading would be fun, and it's not fun." Grace had a master's degree in reading and I was brand-new in first grade. "You know," she said in her quiet way, "there are other programs besides Lippincott. We could go to a reading conference together and look into them." Until that point, I had no idea what a professional conversation looked or sounded like. I suppose, like my children, I needed a scaffold for learning how to speak in this new way.

Suzie   Our arguments that children learn by being invited to participate in an ongoing ritual, or conversation, apply to teachers. Conversation leads to a sense of social responsibility, to a sense of having a powerful brain, to a mutual interest in exploring the unknown, and ultimately to agreed-on action.

I thought of Sheri and the other children who came back from the sixth grade to conduct a conversation about the gun incident at the middle school. In their eyes they had a responsibility, so they acted. They came, moved the chairs into position, and began to talk, one as the leader inviting the others to participate. Such a conversation was nothing new; they had carried on many discussions on the rug in Suzanne's class. They knew how to do this. "We've come," Sheri said. "We have to do this."

Action doesn't have to come at the end of the line when everybody is smart enough; it's a means as well as an end. That's why both children and teachers should be put in charge of their conversations, even when they're still beginners. The children who came back to Suzanne's room to pull their chairs together and say, "I have something to say," had had plenty of practice in speaking, responding, and thinking actively. They had practiced all the way from day one.

The bad news is that teachers typically do not have this practice.

Suzanne   And why not? Why, for example, do they not use teacher meetings as opportunities to converse about teaching? Why do they not take charge of these conversations?

Let me tell you. School is a hierarchical affair. The status of the teacher is low. A teacher's status improves as she or he moves out of the classroom—into the reading specialist's office, the library, the principal's office. Such moves are referred to as "moving up." So what typically happens in meetings between teachers and other people in the school system is that teachers take on the traditional role of the student. They answer questions, but they don't ask their own. They don't initiate topics for discussion. Like students, they act out their subordinate roles.

Suzie   Tracy Kidder, in his book *Among Schoolchildren* (1989), shows in chilling detail how the hierarchical style of a teachers' meeting in an elementary school prevents teachers from bringing up problems. Chris Zajac, the teacher at the center of this book, has had trouble teaching math to her fifth grade. She has several children like Charles the ghost and Arthur the cheater. She looks energetically for ideas. She wants to improve. She improvises children's drama in the classroom. She exhorts the children to excellence with all the fervor of a battlefield commander. Yet, when the textbook representative is invited to talk with the faculty about math, she attends the meeting out of duty. Like the rest of the teachers, she looks passively at the overhead projector and lets the speaker's jargon slide by. The faculty members sitting near her whisper but ask no questions. Chris and a teacher friend giggle behind their hands.

There is no room, within the controlling discourse of the teacher meeting, for the real conversation Chris would like to have. She can raise her hand and be called on, but the conventions tell her she has no business bringing up her problems.

Suzanne   There are times, because the school is hierarchical like the classroom, when administrators should set up small-group teacher meetings and then stay out. Children meeting without me in small groups were more intellectually active than children whom I "helped" by sitting in. Teachers, likewise, take on greater responsibility when they're in charge of their conversations.

A story now circulates in my school about a group of fifth-grade teachers who repeatedly asked to meet with the sixth-grade teachers at the middle school. The fifth-grade teachers clamored for the meeting. They wanted it to talk over some problems of great concern. But when all of the teachers were finally assembled, after months had been spent trying to find a time in everybody's tight schedule, they were faced by a curriculum supervisor who stood by the chalkboard issuing directions. "Write answers to my questions," she said, "on these yellow sticky notes. Then post them on the bulletin board. You may direct general questions to me, and I will write them on the board."

"When do we talk?" asked a teacher.

"Oh, this is not a meeting to talk," she said. "This is a meeting to decide what we will talk about if we have a meeting to talk."

Suzie And then what happened?

Suzanne The teachers did as they were told. Most of the meeting time was taken up following the directives. Then everyone went home. Time passed. They never did have the meeting to talk about whatever it was they were going to talk about.

   The moral, I think, is that teachers shouldn't go to a meeting expecting a conversation. Meetings don't work that way because the very word *meeting* says administration, directives, and control. You can hardly have a meeting where the teachers are in charge of the conversation.

Suzie What, then, if not meetings?

   As we talked, Suzanne and I began to list all of the various professional conversations from which we had learned lessons of value in our careers: national conferences with thousands of teachers in attendance, our own one-to-one chats, Suzanne's conversations with Marilyn and Ellen, her discussions with other teachers whom she mentored, an occasional graduate course or workshop, and all her summer project study sessions, including the Maui symposium.

   Our question, we finally decided, was a question about scaffolding: Can these existing forums become scaffolds for teacher dialogue? As we talked, we returned to the idea of chapter 2—the idea of school culture and its influence on the patterns of talk. There was no lack of programs to teach teachers and reteach them, but, as might be expected, the people running these programs carry on in the ways they themselves were taught. It was the school culture perpetuating itself. Frequently, teachers were gathered together and lectured to. But they were given little chance to debate issues or contribute to a discussion that might lead to action on their part.

   Supposing we could design our own scaffold for initiating new teachers into professional conversations, what should the scaffolder do? What principles should the scaffolder follow to put teachers in charge of the conversation?

Those principles, it seemed to us, could be found in the earlier chapters of this book. Suzanne and I now made a list of several that we discovered there, putting them in the form of advice to those who saw themselves as scaffolders. Here is the list:

The Principle of Real Questions. Real questions are the learner's own questions. Wait for these. Establish a conversational atmosphere in which the real can be turned into the good.

The Principle of Stories. Many real questions derive from stories told by learners. Provide time for these.

The Principle of Writing Together. Learners learn courtesy and empathy when they write together and share their words. Use writing as a way for learners to generate their thoughts, then contribute them to the group.

The Principles of Response, Reflection, and Revision. Writers look back to see what they have said. They listen to response. They revise. Learners need time, whether writing or not, to reflect on what they have said, listen to response, and revise. Provide conversational ways (in speech or writing) for learners to do so.

The Principle of the Common Good. The wagon train, the journey in the company of others, the team—all of these are metaphors for valuing "the common good" and scaffolding the helping relationship. Use and teach a metaphor of this kind. Create a consciousness of shared purpose.

The Principle of Multiple and Shared Authority. No one has all the right answers. Everybody has some of them. Lead learners to credit interactive processes of inquiry and to examine the concept of authority.

The Principle of Doubt and Discomfort. In a conversational atmosphere, learners such as Larry can tolerate and even entertain, doubt. Children can (sometimes) knock whole walls of their stories down, once they learn to accept the destruction that accompanies change. Encourage learners to welcome temporary discomfort as a price of change, development, or new knowledge.

The Principle of Crossing Boundaries. Sheri crossed institutional boundaries—from middle to elementary school—to take responsible action. Suzanne and I have crossed the boundaries between university and school. What we have discovered this way has been for us enormously rewarding. Encourage learners to seek the perspective of people on the other side of the boundary.

Suzanne   As Suzie and I put this list of principles together, we chatted about the Central California Writing Project, which in my case had been a classic scaffold. I realize now that without this supportive structure, my conversation with Marilyn and Ellen—even the one with Suzie—would never have materialized. I probably would never have done the taping project nor gone to conferences to present the results. My first summer with the writing project in Santa Cruz in 1979 showed me how to carry on a professional conversation.

There, in Santa Cruz, I found myself outside of the school hierarchy. I wasn't being "inserviced." I was not being talked down to. I was credited with having intelligence and made responsible. I was teaching myself by teaching others, who in this project happened to be a group of university and high school writing teachers. I was one of only two teachers from the elementary level, so it was clear that aside from one other person, I knew more about teaching elementary school than anyone else in the project, including Don Rothman, the project director. I had a measure of authority.

Yet during the time of the institute, doubt and discomfort were daily companions. At the end of every day I'd come back to my little room on campus and say to myself, "What was that all about? This is fun but why on earth am I here?" So then I thought, "They're talking about high school, but it's not just high school." For five intense weeks I mused and meditated.

My head swam in ideas. I was reading Maxine Hairston about writing process and the paradigm shift. I read James Britton and

Nancy Martin, whom I liked because they were talking about children and schools. I read Elbow and Shaughnessy. I read Marie Clay and all sorts of things about early childhood, early speech, and early writing, which was exciting. Then Don would say, "Here's something by James Moffett" and "Here's something else that's wonderful," and all the time I was reacting: "This I like" and "This is opposite to what I'm doing." So I was taking in a vast number of ways to think about writing.

But I was doing more than taking in. In the company of others, joined together in a common pursuit, I began to ask my real questions. Writing helped me to do this, because it gave me the space to think, and writing together gave me people to explain things to. The small-group meetings worked wonderfully; we all rose to the occasion somehow, taking every question seriously. The very fact that I was practically the only elementary teacher—the fact of having to talk to people every day who came from a wholly different perspective—meant that I could no longer ask myself, "What will I do tomorrow in the classroom?" Now I had to ask the larger question "What will I do and why?" That question—Why?—is the one that bound all of us together.

The writing project came at a perfect time in my professional life; it gave me support while I wrestled with ideas.

Suzie   What about my own university classes? What about ongoing seminars offered by the local school district, or mentoring programs, or the state office of education? Can they scaffold teacher conversations? Certainly they can.

But all of these forums, I thought, could take a lesson from the organization and style of the writing project in Santa Cruz. The project offered support. It offered community and the opportunity to act in this community. It empowered people. It was a conversational ritual that invited people in while teaching a sense of how to care, how to think of the common good.

I saw all this in the summer of 1990, when Suzanne went back to Santa Cruz and I joined her, four days a week for four weeks.

Every morning for those four weeks the two of us drove from her house in Carmel to the Santa Cruz campus, taking a route she had traveled so often enroute to writing projects in years past, that she knew it like the back of her hand. No need to worry about direction, she said, we could lose ourselves completely in conversation. The car would drive itself past the dunes and the ice plant along the coast, past the live bait shop, past the Watsonville turn off, straight into Santa Cruz, then up the long hill to the forest of redwoods and the gnarled oaks of Oakes College.

In the classroom on the first day, two tables were a jumble of cups, coffee maker, fresh strawberries, bagels, and cream cheese, which had been brought by Don. Tomasita volunteered to bring food the next day, Roger the next, and so it began, the rituals of turn taking that would characterize the sharing of both food and thought over the next four weeks.

The first activity every day was the convening ritual. Don played convenor on the first day. He spent his fifteen minutes talking about teacher research, read a bit from an article, and wondered aloud how his own work fitted the definition and how it might fit the work that all of us were doing. He passed out an anthology of teacher-written articles, invited us to read anything and everything we found interesting, then suggested that we write for ten minutes, thinking and reacting on paper.

The ten-minute writing was part of the ritual. So was the hour's discussion that followed. By the time I joined the project, Suzanne, Lisa, Ginny, Ellen, Nancy, and the rest had all done at least another summer's work, so they were used to Don's routine. As for me, the years of writing group meetings had made me aware that what I was witnessing that first day had a tacit structure. The rules of courtesy were strict but at the same time invitational. We took turns responding, sometimes reading aloud our pieces of writing, sometimes not. In responding, we usually referred to another speaker's words, sometimes in the manner of "your words reminded me of." No one told us in what order to speak. No one seemed bothered by the silences between speakers. No one felt called on to say, "I think what you're saying is . . ."

Since 1990, Suzanne and I have continued to meet each summer with the same group, four days only but long enough to re-establish the routine. (The California members get together for one-day sessions three or four other days in the year, though I, alas, cannot make these sessions.) The conversation is stimulating. We might arrive tired, but we leave charged up. The rules of courtesy and respect are as comfortable as an easy chair. As with Sheri returning to Suzanne's classroom, I find it completely natural to pull into the circle and say, with authority, "I have something to say and I'm here to say it."

Suzanne   Neither one of us wants to miss a project session because we want to hear how everyone's work is going. Last summer we saw Sylvia and Ruby's video of Hispanic parents holding meetings in the school to discuss themselves, their children, and literacy. We read Debbi and Sarah-Hope's article on bilingual writing and cross-age tutoring. We heard about writing in Guatemala from Karen, and from Nancy about writing and the problems of homophobia in California high schools. Right now Don's in the middle of an interview project, a collaboration between himself and his writing students, so we want to hear how that turns out.

Going around the circle, you hear everyone's story. It works the same with teachers as it does with children. The air grows heavy with empathy as people listen. It's important in my classroom that all of the children tell their stories, and the same goes for members of the professional community. We must all speak.

Suzie   When teachers have a conversational relationship with the others in their professional community, and when the structures for periodic meeting, reading, writing, and conversation are in place, then teachers behave much as the children did from Suzanne's class. They feel authority. They take responsibility for granted. They act. Responsible and creative classroom change is pushed along, like water in a stream, by the currents of professional conversation.

Currents don't stop. Conversations don't finish. They continue on, perhaps slowing with the conditions of the time, but then resuming with the change of seasons and the flow of ideas.

Suzanne We see no reason why this one should stop just because we've come to the end of the print on the page. Our teaching practices will surely continue to evolve and change. Tomorrow we'll have more questions.

To our readers, we extend an invitation to join us. There's space here. Jot a few words. Talk to each other. Talk with us. Send us a line or converse with us at a teacher conference. The pleasure would be ours entirely.

References

Activity Resources Co., Inc. P.O. Box 4875, Hayward, CA 94545

Adams, Alison K. 1990. "Classifier as Apprentice." *The Quarterly Newsletter of the Laboratory of Comparative Human Cognition* 12:76–79. San Diego, CA: University of California, San Diego, Center for Human Information Processing.

Adams, Alison K. & Donald Bullock. 1986. "Apprenticeship in Word Use: Social Convergence Processes in Learning Categorically Related Nouns." *The Development of Word Meaning*. eds. S.A. Kuczaj, II & M.D. Barrett. New York: Springer-Verlag.

Alexander, Lloyd. 1985. *Time Cat*. New York: Dell.

Andersen, Hans Christian. 1985. *Snow Queen*. Trans. Eva Le Gallienne. New York: Harper Children's Books.

Armstrong, William H. 1972. *Sounder*. New York: HarperCollins Children's Books.

Aukerman, Robert C. 1981. *The Basal Reader Approach to Reading*. New York: Wiley.

Avi. 1987. *The Fighting Ground*. New York: Harper Children's Books.

———. 1990. *True Confessions of Charlotte Doyle*. New York: Orchard Books.

Babbitt, Natalie. 1975. *Tuck Everlasting*. New York: Farrar, Straus, & Giroux.

———. 1990. "Protecting Children's Literature: On Preserving the Fragile Medium of Fiction." *The Horn Book Magazine*.

Banks, Lynne Reid. 1985. *Indian in the Cupboard*. New York: Doubleday.

Barr, Mary A. 1988. *Implementing a Research-Based Curriculum in English-Language-Arts, K–12*. State Staff Development and Curriculum Conference. Sacramento, CA: California State Department of Education.

Bateson, Mary Catherine. 1989. *Composing a Life*. New York: Atlantic Monthly Press.

Baum, L. Frank. 1986. *The Wonderful Wizard of Oz.* Berkeley, CA: University of California Press.

Bayer, Ann S. 1990a. "University Students as Apprentice Thinkers." *The Quarterly Newsletter of the Laboratory of Comparative Human Cognition.* 12:64–69. San Diego, CA: University of California, San Diego, Center for Human Information Processing.

———. 1990b. *Cognitive-Apprenticeship Learning: Language and Thinking Across the Curriculum.* Mountain View, CA: Mayfield Publishing.

Benson, Nancy L. 1979. "The Effects of Peer Feedback During the Writing Process on Writing Performance, Revision, Behavior, and Attitude Toward Writing." Ph.D. diss., University of Colorado at Boulder.

Bigham, Diane. 1985. "Where in the World is Carmen San Diego?" San Rafael, CA: Broderbund Software Inc.

Blanchard, Robert. 1976. *Graphiti: First Quadrant.* Hayward, CA: Activity Resources.

Bloom, Benjamin S., ed. 1956. *Taxonomy of Educational Objectives: The Classification of Educational Goals, Handbook I.* New York: David McKay.

Blume, Judy. 1981. *Superfudge.* New York: Dell.

Boss, Roberta S. 1987. "Peer Group Critiques in Formative Evaluation of College Composition." Ph.D. diss., University of Maryland, College Park.

Brady, Suzanne. 1982. *Flight: Writing for a Classroom Reading Project.* Produced and directed by Fred Grossberg. Urbana, IL: National Council of Teachers of English. Videocassette.

Brady, Suzanne & Suzanne Jacobs. 1988. "Children Responding to Children: Writing Groups and Classroom Community." *Understanding Writing: Ways of Observing, Learning, and Teaching K–8.* 2nd ed. eds. Thomas Newkirk & Nancie Atwell. Portsmouth, NH: Heinemann.

Brandt, Mary E. 1990. "Getting Social About Critical Thinking: Power and Constraints of Apprenticeship." *The Quarterly Newsletter of the Laboratory of Comparative Human Cognition* 12:56–63. San Diego, CA: University of California, San Diego, Center for Human Information Processing.

———. 1991. "Reading and Driving: A Revealing Analogy." *The Kame-hameha Journal of Education* 2:1–8.

Brewton, Sara Westbrook, ed. 1969. *Shrieks at Midnight: Macabre Poems, Eerie and Humorous.* New York: Harper Children's Books.

Britton, James. 1993. *Language and Learning.* 2nd ed. Portsmouth, NH: Boynton/Cook.

Britton, James, Anthony Burgess, Nancy Martin, Alex McLeod, & Harold Rosen. 1975. *The Development of Writing Abilities,* 11–18. London: Macmillan.

Cazden, Courtney. 1988. *Classroom Discourse.* Portsmouth, NH: Heine-mann.

Clay, Marie. 1975. *What Did I Write?* Portsmouth, NH: Heinemann.

Cleary, Beverly. 1984. *Dear Mr. Henshaw.* New York: Dell.

———. 1985. *Ramona Forever.* New York: Dell.

Cohen, Elizabeth. 1986. *Designing Group Work: Strategies for the Hetero-geneous Classroom.* New York: Teachers College Press.

Collier, James Lincoln & Christopher Collier. 1985. *My Brother Sam is Dead.* New York: Scholastic.

Crowhurst, Marion. 1979. "The Writing Workshop: An Experiment in Peer Response to Writing." *Language Arts* 56:757–62.

Day, Veronique. 1972. *Landslide!* New York: Dell.

Dynamath. New York: Scholastic.

Eckert, Allan W. 1972. *Incident at Hawk's Hill.* New York: Dell.

Educational Oasis. Carthage, IL: Good Apple.

Elbow, Peter. 1973. *Writing Without Teachers.* New York: Oxford Univer-sity Press.

Elbow, Peter & Patricia Belanoff. 1989. *A Community of Writers.* New York: McGraw-Hill.

Emig, Janet. 1971. *The Composing Processes of Twelfth Graders.* Urbana, IL: National Council of Teachers of English.

Fast, Howard. 1983. *April Morning.* New York: Bantam Books.

Fitzgerald, John D. 1972. *Great Brain.* New York: Dell.

Forbes, Esther. 1969. *Johnny Tremain.* New York: Dell.

Ford, Bob W. 1973. "The Effects of Peer Editing/Grading on the Grammar—Usage and Theme—Composition Ability of College Freshmen." Ph.D. diss., University of Oklahoma, Norman.

Freedman, Sarah W. 1987. *Response to Student Writing.* Urbana, IL: National Council of Teachers of English.

Fritz, Jean. 1982. *Can't You Make Them Behave, King George?* New York: Putnam.

Gardner, Howard. 1983. *Frames of Mind: The Theory of Multiple Intelligences.* New York: Basic Books.

George, Jean C. 1988. *My Side of the Mountain.* New York: Dutton Children's Books.

Gere, Anne Ruggles. 1987. *Writing Groups: History, Theory and Implications.* Carbondale: Southern Illinois University Press.

Glaze, Bernedette, Carin M. Hauser, & Christopher Thaiss. 1987. "What Happens When Students Write Learning Logs as Third Graders, as Tenth Graders, as Sophomores in College." Presentation for the annual meeting of the National Council of Teachers of English.

Goffman, Erving. 1972. *Frame Analysis.* Los Angeles: University of California Press.

Goodlad, John. 1984. *A Place Called School.* New York: McGraw-Hill.

Goodman, Kenneth S. 1965. "A Linguistic Study of Cues and Miscues in Reading." *Elementary English* 42:639–43.

Goodman, Kenneth S. & Yetta Goodman. 1979. "Learning to Read is Natural." *Theory and Practice of Early Reading.* Vol. 1. eds. L.B. Resnick & P.A. Weaver. Hillsdale, NJ: Erlbaum.

Goodman, Kenneth S., Patrick Shannon, Yvonne Freeman, & Sharon Murphy. 1988. *Report Card on Basal Readers.* Katonah, NY: Richard C. Owen.

Gould, Stephen J. 1981. *The Mismeasure of Man.* New York: Norton.

Graves, Donald. 1983. *Writing: Teachers and Children at Work.* Portsmouth, NH: Heinemann.

Hairston, Maxine. 1982. "The Winds of Change: Thomas Kuhn and the Revolution in the Teaching of Writing." *College Composition and Communication* 33:76–88.

Harnadek, Anita. 1979. *Warm-Up Mind Benders.* Pacific Grove, CA: Midwest Publications.

History-Social Science Framework for California Public Schools. 1988. Sacramento, CA: California State Department of Education.

Howgate, Lynn. 1983. *Building Self-Esteem Through the Writing Process.* Berkeley, CA: National Writing Project.

Huang, Su-yueh. n.d. "Learning to Critique in Peer Response Groups in an ESL University Writing Class." Ph.D. diss., University of Hawaii.

Instructor. New York: Scholastic.

Jacobs, Suzanne E. 1984. "Investigative Writing: Practice and Principles." *Language Arts* 61:356–63.

———. 1990. "Scaffolding Children's Consciousness as Thinkers." *The Quarterly Newsletter of the Laboratory of Comparative Human Cognition* 12:70–75. San Diego, CA: University of California, San Diego, Center for Human Information Processing.

Jacobs, Suzanne E. & Adela B. Karliner. 1977. "Helping Writers to Think: The Effect of Speech Roles in Individual Conferences on the Quality of Thought in Student Writing." *College English* 38:489–505.

Karengianes, Myra L., Ernest T. Pascarella, & Susanna W. Pflaum. 1980. "The Effects of Peer-Editing on the Writing Proficiency of Low-Achieving Tenth Grade Students." *The Journal of Educational Research* 73:203–207.

Kidder, Tracy. 1989. *Among Schoolchildren.* Boston: Houghton Mifflin.

L'Engle, Madeleine. 1976. *A Wrinkle in Time.* New York: Dell.

Levin, Paula F. 1990. "Culturally Contextualized Apprenticeship: Teaching and Learning through Helping in Hawaiian Families." *The Quarterly Newsletter of the Laboratory of Comparative Human Cognition* 12:80–85. San Diego, CA: University of California, San Diego, Center for Human Information Processing.

Levin, Paula F., Mary E. Brenner, & J. Mahealani McClellan. 1987. "Schooling and the Transformation of Pacific Societies." Unpublished paper. Honolulu, HI: Kamehameha Schools, Center for Development of Early Education.

Lord, Bette Bao. 1986. *In the Year of the Boar and Jackie Robinson.* New York: HarperCollins Children's Books.

Lowry, Lois. 1990. *Number the Stars.* New York: Dell.

McPeck, John E. 1981. *Critical Thinking and Education.* New York: St. Martin's Press.

Moffett, James. 1983. *Teaching the Universe of Discourse.* Portsmouth, NH: Boynton/Cook.

Montgomery, L. M. 1989. *Anne of Green Gables.* New York: Scholastic.

Morison, Kay & Suzanne Brady. 1994. HOMEWORK! Bridging the Gap Between School and Home. Kirkland, WA: Goodfellow Press.

Murray, Donald. 1979. "The Listening Eye: Reflections on the Writing Conference." *College English* 41:13–18.

Neill, Alexander S. 1960. *Summerhill.* New York: Hart Publishing.

Newkirk, Thomas. 1989. *More Than Stories: The Range of Children's Writing.* Portsmouth, NH: Heinemann.

Newkirk, Thomas & Nancie Atwell, eds. 1988. *Understanding Writing: Ways of Observing, Learning, and Teaching K–8.* 2nd ed. Portsmouth, NH: Heinemann.

North, Stephen. 1987. *The Making of Knowledge in Composition: Portrait of An Emerging Field.* Portsmouth, NH: Boynton/Cook.

Nystrand, Martin. 1986. "Learning to Write by Talking about Writing: A Summary of Research on Intensive Peer Review in Expository Writing Instruction at the University of Wisconsin, Madison." *The Structure of Written Communication: Studies in Reciprocity between Writers and Readers.* Orlando, FL: Academic Press.

O'Neal, Sharon. 1991. "Leadership in the Language Arts: Student Assessment: Present and Future." *Language Arts* 68:67–73.

Palinscar, Ann & Ann Brown. 1984. "Reciprocal Teaching of Comprehension-Fostering and Comprehension-Monitoring Activities." *Cognition and Instruction* 1:117–75.

Paterson, Katherine. 1987. *Bridge to Terabithia.* New York: Harper-Collins Children's Books.

Paulsen, Gary. 1988. *Hatchet.* New York: Puffin Books.

Rawls, Wilson. 1974. *Where the Red Fern Grows.* New York: Bantam.

Rogoff, Barbara. 1990. *Apprenticeship in Thinking: Cognitive Development in the Social Context.* New York: Oxford University Press.

Rolvaag, O.E. 1991. *Giants in the Earth: A Saga of the Prairie.* New York: HarperCollins.

Russell, Connie. 1985. "Peer Conferencing and Writing Revision: A Study of the Relationship." *Service Bulletin* (48). Wisconsin Council of Teachers of English.

Sager, Carol. 1973. "Improving the Quality of Written Composition through Pupil Use of Rating Scale." Paper presented to the annual meeting of the National Council of Teachers of English. ERIC ED 089 304.

Scardamalia, Marlene, Carl Bereiter, & Roseanne Steinbach. 1984. "Teachability of Reflective Processes in Written Composition." *Cognitive Science* 8:173–90.

Schuman, Kate. 1976. *Monster Math.* Los Angeles, CA: Media for Education.

Scott Foresman Reading Series, Golden Secrets & Scott Foresman Reading Series, Sea Treasures. 1983. Book authors: Richard G. Smith and Robert J. Tierney. Glenview, IL: Scott Foresman.

Scribner, Sylvia. 1990. "Reflections on a Model." *The Quarterly Newsletter of the Laboratory of Comparative Human Cognition.* 12:90–95. San Diego, CA: University of California, San Diego, Center for Human Information Processing.

Searle, Dennis. 1984. "Scaffolding: Who's Building Whose Building?" *Language Arts* 61:480–83.

Shaughnessy, Mina. 1977. *Errors and Expectations.* New York: Oxford University Press.

Slavin, Robert. 1988. *Student Team Learning: An Overview and Practical Guide.* 2nd ed. Washington, DC: National Education Association.

Smith, Frank. 1986. *Insult to Intelligence.* Portsmouth, NH: Heinemann.

Stone, Addison. 1989. "What's Missing in the Metaphor of Scaffolding?" Paper presented to the meeting of the American Education Research Association, Northwestern University.

Stone Soup: The Magazine for Children. Santa Cruz, CA: Children's Art Foundation.

Toulmin, Stephen. 1984. *An Introduction to Reasoning.* New York: Macmillan.

Vygotsky, Lev S. 1962. *Thought and Language*. Cambridge, MA: MIT Press & Wiley.

———. 1978. *Mind in Society: The Development of Higher Psychological Processes*. eds. M. Cole, V. John-Steiner, S. Scribner, & E. Souberman. Cambridge, MA: Harvard University Press.

Watson-Gegeo, Karen A. 1990. "The Social Transfer of Cognitive Skills in Kwara'ae." *The Quarterly Newsletter of the Laboratory of Comparative Human Cognition* 12:86–89. San Diego, CA: University of California, San Diego, Center for Human Information Processing.

Watson-Gegeo, Karen A. & David W. Gegeo. 1986. "The Social World of Kwara'ae Children: Acquisition of Language and Values." *Children's Worlds and Children's Language*. eds. J. Cook-Gumperz, W. Corsaro, & J. Streek. Berlin: Mouton de Gruyter.

Weekly Reader. Middletown, CT: Newfield Publications.

Wesley, John. 1974. *Pioneers*. Lakeside, CA: Interact.

White, E.B. 1973. *The Trumpet of the Swan*. New York: HarperCollins Children's Books.

Wilder, Laura Ingalls. 1971. *The Long Winter*. New York: HarperCollins Children's Books.

Wood, David, Jerome S. Bruner, & Gail Ross. 1976. "The Role of Tutoring in Problem Solving." *Journal of Child Psychology and Psychiatry* 17:89–100.

Yaronczyk, Andrew F. 1990. "An Experimental Study of Writing Collaboration at a Middle School: Its Effects on Overall Writing Quality, Performance, Apprehension, Concepts, and Attitudes." Ph.D. diss., Indiana University of Pennsylvania.

Yumori, Wendie & Katherine Tibbets. 1991. "Practitioners' Perceptions of Transition to Portfolio Assessment." *The Kamehameha Journal of Education* 2:37–46.

Index